Mo̶ ̶ ̶ ̶ ̶LIFE

"Anyone ̶ d Life, for its engrossing ̶ Woman who walks the walk, for its perceptive reflections on the insanities of the industrial/consumer society in which we live, and for the information it provides on emerging alternatives, such as cohousing, slow money, vegetarian and raw foods, permaculture and organic gardening, voluntary simplicity, green building, and much more. This is truly an inspiring and informative book."—**Molly Young Brown, author of *Growing Whole: Self-Realization for the Great Turning***

"Sherry Ackerman offers us thirty-five years of life lived close to the earth, simple and sustainable, yet smart, cosmopolitan, erudite. This book is a rich stew of down-to-earth wisdom and practice, and rigorous philosophical, social, economic, and ecological thought."—**John de Graaf, co-author, *Affluenza: The All-Consuming Epidemic***

"In her latest book, Sherry Ackerman draws on philosophers including Plato, Nietzsche, Heidegger, on her experience in a Vermont communal farm, and on her recent years in California to point to practical ways to create an authentic and meaningful life lived close to nature. Both philosophical and pragmatic at once, *The Good Life* beckons us toward the vital process of cultural regeneration."—**Arthur Versluis, author of *Island Farm, The Mystical State*, and other books**

"In her latest book, Dr. Sherry L. Ackerman has illuminated a path heretofore unrevealed in the treasure trove of manuscripts leading us from the edge of oblivion to a sustainable life. Most fundamentally, she has identified concepts that can transform our dead consumer culture into a living postconsumer society. *The Good Life* shines a streak of light on moving beyond addictive consumerism forever."—**Carol Holst, editor of *Get Satisfied: How Twenty People Like You Found the Satisfaction of Enough***

"Don't sweat the small stuff, but let's start paying attention to the big stuff—a dying planet, a wavering economy, and an unsustainable worldview. In *The Good Life*, Sherry Ackerman exemplifies how sustainable living brings us deeper into our personal authenticity and gives us a glimpse of where to begin, with suggestions on how we too can restore our planet back to vitality and well-being."—**Kristine Carlson, author of *Don't Sweat the Small Stuff for Women* and *Heartbroken Open***

THE GOOD LIFE

How to Create a Sustainable and Fulfilling Lifestyle

Sherry Ackerman

Hermitage
House

Paperback, ISBN 978-0-9846032-0-6

Published by
Hermitage House
3609 North Old Stage Road
Mount Shasta, CA 96067

Book design by David Fideler
www.concordeditorial.com

Contents

Foreword

The good life is more than a yearning for the good, the beautiful, the true. It includes decision, will, determination, and effort, individually and collectively, to be clear regarding the theory as well as successful in practice . . . aiming at that integration of thought, the word and deed which is the expression of wisdom and the basis of serenity and inner peace.

—Scott Nearing

Where does the human heart find its greatest repose and happiness? Within the maelstrom of consumer fetishism and consumptive excess, or in a principled life whose actions are measured in the industrious accumulation of daily joys? The answer arrived at to this inquiry will temper the reader's response to this book.

If your answer is the former, then your consumerist education by mass-media advertising is complete. If you answer the second, or even yearn for such a life, then this book will provide a clear-hearted story of how individual self-introspection twinned with the labor of the hands can fulfill not only one's personal needs but also healthfully affect other's lives, be they human, animal or mineral.

In this saga of Ackerman's subzero mornings in midwinter Vermont,

hours spent in the tending and gathering of foodstuffs for family and
attendant beasts, the quiet satisfaction of a child thanking her for his
upbringing by not only discerning her actions but also decoding the
principles she employed to teach him, and the pasture beauty of a
night with Saturn jewelling Mt. Shasta skies, you will find an individual intelligence searching to plan, build, struggle with, re-envision,
strengthen, and variously evolve a humane good life.

How better to view a book than as a useful tool? I view this volume
as a practical course in radical stability through voluntary simplicity.
Freedom cultivated through a consideration of the tensions between
conditioning and consciousness.

Throughout this book, Ackerman weds the work of the hands
with the considerations of the mind. She demonstrates the useable
vitality of philosophy by taking Heidegger, Plato, and Sartre out to
the woodshed and using them to sharpen the tools properly. They
take an edge, and as with any well-cared for tool, the work goes easier
and with greater purpose.

How better to view a book than as a useful tool? I view this volume
as a practical course in radical stability through voluntary simplicity.
Freedom cultivated through a consideration of the tensions between
conditioning and consciousness.

The late-empiric United States juggernaut that threatens to complete
its subconscious terminator-like mission can only be turned from its
apocalypse by the concerted response of communal individualism,
what Victor Turner terms "an independent domain of creative activity." Does this seem woefully inadequate to meet our present situation? Certainly, but what other course is left to us? And what other
course could fulfill our visions beyond a welter of market necessities,
collateralized debt obligations, and the stagnation of enforced unem-
ployable redundancy.

To this end Ackerman unthreads the beliefs that drive our internal calculus concerning time, money, and wealth, then proceeds to
examine how she reconstructed her own internal mindscape so as to
be able to see the "world" more clearly and thus be able to interact
with it on a deeper and more health-fulfilling manner.

Yes, yes, I hear you say, but what does he mean? Take horse bedding. The expense of it. The faults inherent in various materials. Now
take the keenness of a self-disciplined thinker who has incubated a

program of rational thought. Ackerman sees the waste paper generated at a local college, carts the "waste" home, beds her horse in it who voids his waste onto it, which she then cures into the world's true gold—compost.

If we cannot find such creative ways of dealing with our daily "wastes," then we will allow the juggernaut to carry us into the chaotic abyss of environmental collapse. In the exercise of *urine mindfulness,* Ackerman shows us how to see where we are so that we can decide what direction is truly in the best interest of ourselves and nature, rather than what is economically expedient.

Thoreau observed: "Is not the poet bound to write his own biography? We do not wish to know how his imaginary hero, but how he, the actual hero, lived from day to day" (October 21, 1857). Excepting the gender, how well this applies to Ackerman's work. Here we have an honest, forthright, detailed, considerate, philosophical manual and biography that provides the reader with not *the* good life, but *a* Good Life.

This is not a manual on how to live your life, but a concordance of ideas and processes by which you can envision a new lifeway in a practicable manner: a culturing of the soul that provides us the possibility of a transformed social structure just when the horizon seems, if not downright uglified, bleak. Dumas wrote, "The soul forms its own horizons." Sherry L. Ackerman has revealed the astromechanics of her journey so as to assist us in our own cross-grained, yet ultimately rewarding, lifelong epoch traversal.

—Greg Joly
Maynard Hollow, Vermont
May Day 2010

Introduction

*The good life is never stable, never secure, never easy
and never ended. It is a series of steps or stages, one
leading into the other and all, in their outcome,
adding, not subtracting; augmenting, not diminishing;
building, not destroying; creating, not annihilating.*

—Scott and Helen Nearing

A leaf fell softly from one of the big oak trees today when I was
outside turning my garden. It still had a little green left around the
veins, but was mostly yellow with hints of crimson. I paused and
savored the moment. I felt grateful for my good life: a tapestry of
simple pleasures. It's been two years since the 2008 economic crash.
For many Americans, these have been the hardest years of their lives.
They have lost jobs, homes, retirement funds, income, and investments.
Many are servicing so much debt-load that they feel oppressed by
their own lives.

My pantry and freezer are full of the produce from this summer's
garden and the woodpile is stacked. I am in excellent health from
riding my bicycle to town and back, in the fresh air and sunshine, for
errands. There is plenty of new hay, for which I bartered, in the barn

to feed the horses over the winter. I remember my grandmother talking about living through the Great Depression. She looked into the distance with a faint smile on her lips, reminiscing about raising her small children on a subsistence farm during the rockiest of financial times that America, at that time, had ever seen. She recalled, "We barely knew that the Depression was going on" as she recounted how their lifestyle had buffered them from hardship. Today, we would call their subsistence farm a *sustainable farm*—or a permaculture venture. In many ways, my lifestyle has been an incremental reversion, over the years, to that of my grandparents.

The blueprint drawn by Scott and Helen Nearing also helped forge my own life path. So, when the markets fell in 2008—with the subsequent waves of foreclosures, layoffs, and monetary devaluation—like my grandmother and the Nearings—I was insulated. The lifestyle I had created for myself over the past twenty-five years was sustainable: voluntarily simple and purposeful. My fertile, organic gardens, animal husbandry skills, and practice of living simply on the land provided me with freedom from anxiety and tension and an opportunity to live harmoniously in an increasingly complicated world. My life has taught me that contemporary consumer culture inflames the hunting-and-gathering instinct beyond *need,* and even beyond *wanting.* It fosters an addiction to wanting and greed for which the correction might only be to move away from induced neediness towards the sanity of satiety—to move away from the peripatetic search for "more" towards "enough."

Americans are subconsciously driven by a perverted interpretation of social Darwinism that assumes that survival is necessarily competitive. The feminine archetype, preferring cooperation, has been reduced to a mere concept in the pace of the contemporary fast lane. The ego, terrified of annihilation, rushes toward its own survival at the expense of others and the earth. Our souls—our most essential nature—aren't concerned with survival. Our souls are immortal and eternal, and somewhere—buried underneath all of the noise in our heads—we know that. It is the ego that fights to survive. It hangs on for dear life. It also pushes, tramples, scrambles and batters its way to more, more, more. It never has enough. Big business plays on the ego's lust. When the ego wants more, the products are there to buy.

Somewhere along the way, the lines between democracy and capitalism got very blurry. And, when they did, citizens turned into consumers. People were no longer members of an interconnected social fabric, known as community, but became cogs in the wheels of an ever-expanding economic system. This is the way we have done business for decades. But recent events have made it overtly obvious that, unlike the farm, it is not sustainable. We, can't, as a culture, just go back to business as usual. This time, we have to create something new. This is a turning point.

The recent market crash, while not without its share of heart-breaking stories, offers Americans an opportunity. It offers the opportunity to make a course correction that would allow people to take their lives into their own hands and live in a simpler, less routinized, more socially sensible manner. Right now, there is an option available: to exchange high-rises and fluorescent lights, suburbs and office cubicles, processed air, food and water, keeping up with the proverbial Joneses, and those ubiquitous racing rats equipped with cell phones and beepers, with feeling the sun or the wind and rain on our faces, organic garden produce in our bellies, and a much slower pace of life. There is growing interest in becoming freed from consumerism while still being an active participant in society. People are thinking about reclaiming themselves as citizens instead of as consumers.

Changing from a "market economy," which, in the words of the Nearings, "seeks by ballyhoo to bamboozle consumers into buying things they neither need nor want, thus compelling them to sell their labor power as a means of paying for their purchases" to a "use economy," in which there is an integrated balance of good friends, live soil, social awareness, vital food, and recreation, would promote active participation in the advancement of social justice, creative integration of the life of the mind, body and spirit, and deliberate choice in living responsibly. Twenty-first century pioneers can make a choice to craft a lifestyle that honors work, viewing it as one aspect of the self-development process, without denying time for contemplation or recreation.

The recent global markets' downturn is an opportunity to reintegrate with our most essential selves. It is a time, not without some suffering, that we could step outside of our roles and inhabit our souls. It's about not viewing wealth as money, but as something much more holistic and broad. Yes, this book is about my own journey to sustainability—getting outside of the box and being more authentically human. But it's not just my journey: it's one that anyone can choose. Each person has to make their own map, find their own way. My work has broken open the ground before you as surely as if I'd gotten up a little earlier than you did and, forceful in the powerful morning light, turned over a garden of healthy, vital soil. It's all there for you, ready, if you choose to dig and plant.

1

Condemned to Be Free

Man is condemned to be free; because once thrown into the world, he is responsible for everything he does.

—Jean-Paul Sartre

We were drinking some good espresso in an outdoor café when my grown son, Pher, turned to me and said, "You know, Mom, it was only recently that I realized that we lived the way that we did when I was kid *by choice*. I mean, I had always thought that we were poor." I grinned and asked him to say more. "Well, it was just so different. I mean, when I compared my life to other kids at school, there was such a huge difference—and I just figured that we lived that way because we had to. I had no idea that you and Dad—well, that you and Dad had actively chosen that lifestyle." "What made you realize it?" I asked, curious. "Well, now that I'm an adult myself, I have more of an insight into lifestyle differences—and personal finances. It's obvious to me that you are not poor. In fact, you're not poor at all! But you still keep the same lifestyle. So I put two and two together and it all began to make sense."

"When I talk to other people my age, they don't believe me when I tell them about my childhood. They think I'm making it up." I took a long breath and asked him what he thought about his child-hood. His reply surprised me. "It was the absolute best childhood that a person could have. I will never forget it and I cherish every memory." I mumbled something about there not being any adequate training for parenting and apologized for all of the foibles that his Dad and I had made. He got big, red-faced, and vehement, and said, "Don't ever say that again. You gave me the greatest gift that anyone could ever be given. I had an amazing upbringing." I walked out of the café with a lot to think about. He had been really passion-ate. There was an authenticity in his tone that pushed my process.

I kept thinking about Pher's comments as I bicycled home. I stopped a couple of times en route and picked some red clover to dry for winter tea. But my thoughts were not on what I was doing. I kept drifting back to those years on a back-to-the-earth commune in Central Vermont where Pher and his sister, Jec, had been born in the mid-1970s. I had moved to "the farm," as it came to be called, on the flip of a coin—literally. I had just finished graduate school during the heyday of the American cultural revolution. We were the generation of students confronted with the Vietnam war, racial tension, second-wave feminism, and runaway capitalism. Fritjof Capra hadn't yet written *The Turning Point* and we weren't sure there was much hope in sight. Things seemed pretty incongruous.

I had tried working at a straight job, with that brand new Ph.D. hanging after my name, but learned that nine to five wasn't going to cut it for me. I needed a life—I mean, a real life, one in which I *lived,* not just *worked.* The only thing that seemed coherent was Nature—the land, animals, the seasons and mountains. I was in love with mountains. The time was ripe for back-to-the-earth communes, and a lot of my peers were heading to places like California, Colorado, and New Mexico. I was attracted to the Great Smokey Mountains in Tennessee and the Green Mountains of Vermont. So I flipped a coin and Vermont won the flip. The rest is my story. I packed my meager belongings and headed to the North Woods.

1974: On an Old Farm in Vermont

Things fell in place, like they tend to do when you're in the Flow, and I landed at an old, run-down, one-hundred-and-fifty acre farm smack dab in the middle of the Green Mountain State. The year was 1974, and for the next twenty-two years, I called a two-hundred-year-old farmhouse, located eleven miles out on a minimally maintained gravel road, home. A lot happened for me there. I got married, had two children, and forged my way into an equestrian career that has given me an incredibly good life. And, of course, I taught philosophy—which I can't seem to outrun—at an area university. But those things are really the least of it. They were just the outer garments of a more important inner journey that took place. What really happened for me there was transformation—deep, lasting, and significant. The woman who walked off that place twenty-two years later was a whole different person than the one who had gone there in 1974.

I'd gone to graduate school in South Carolina. That meant that my wardrobe didn't have long sleeves and, more to the point, certainly didn't include long johns. That all changed very quickly. I remember the first time I stepped out onto the front porch of that old Vermont farmhouse and the hairs inside my nostrils froze solid. I couldn't figure out why, since the thermometer registered thirty degrees. My then-husband, a native Vermonter, laughingly pointed out that those thirty degrees were on the sub side of zero. In that moment, I got a glimpse of what lay ahead. I also got my first clue that I probably didn't have sufficient skill to negotiate this new lifestyle—that a really steep learning curve was just over the horizon.

We all dressed like Marxists in those days, with combat boots and long flannel skirts—an outfit that, fortunately, accommodated doubling up underneath with insulated long johns. People probably thought that the flannel bandanas wrapped around our heads were a hippy fashion statement, when it was much more about the fact that 75 percent of our body heat was escaping out of our heads and that we were desperate to preserve those BTUs. This simple event, though, was symbolic of the shift that I went through on the farm. My whole life, one thing at a time, stopped being about mere appearances and started being geared toward sensibility and sustainability. Like the consummate Platonist, I knew that Socrates considered the unexamined life not worth living. Now I stood on the threshold of experiencing "an examined life."

At the time, in my incredible naivety, it sounded plausible. Perhaps even simple. I would simply deconstruct all of my social and cultural conditioning and there I would be, nakedly authentic. The whole vision had a distinctively Heideggerian[1] flavor. I set out to repossess my life, to wrench myself away from the cultural "they." I was not going to settle for being *das Man*. I was going to rise above my enculturation. Heidegger's big idea was that most people get so lost in being *das Man* that they never engage in real discourse, being content, instead, with idle chatter—groundless, buzzing talk that focuses on reaching a superficial consensus instead of exploring anything new. At the farm, this came to be referred to as "banter" and we tried to sidestep it. We were going to go deep, and that kind of interpersonal excavation started with our thoughts and our speech.

As time went by, my own existential crisis became more and more evident. I had been born into a world of quiet conformity. Raised on Ozzie and Harriet, Father Knows Best, and Car 54 in front of an old black and white TV set, most of what I said, thought, and believed was some variation of the standard cultural myth. My mother had been the consummate materialist—which had probably inadvertently sent me running in the opposite direction. As a child, I was uneasy with her lust for profit and gain. I felt as if there was something dreadfully wrong with her life—which was singularly dominated by her money and her "stuff"—and knew that I was looking for something different.

Most of the activities, though, that I regarded worthy of my time and effort, the ultimate values that I pursued, and the particular styles and forms through which I planned to pursue these goals—even though apparently countercultural—had still all sprung from various societal expectations. It was becoming obvious that I was wrapped in a cultural cocoon of conformity and inauthenticity, and that radical individuation presented the only possibility of emergence. My naivety was shattered—so much for the fast track to naked authenticity.

2010: At a Philosophical Hermitage in California

Fast forward thirty-five years. These days, I live at the foot of Mount Shasta, in California, at a quiet philosophical Hermitage with Philosopher King, Daniel Kealey. We both arrived here in ongoing process of discovering who we are. Existential transients, I suppose. Kealey is from the Netherlands and is the quintessential European city boy. And if you're getting the idea that I came with Vermont topsoil under my fingernails and Plato's *Dialogues* stuck in the pocket of a pair of overalls, that is correct. Each of us had left our marriages in order to pursue opportunities for deeper spiritual and psychological growth. We had, though, taken incredibly different paths to arrive here. While I had unfolded with my feet either in the soil or jammed in a pair of stirrups, Kealey had spent the same amount of time as an ivory tower academician. He had written *Revisioning Environmental Ethics* during the same time period I had lived it. So when we put our lives together, concept walked beside experience.

Anyway, one day, as Kealey sat outside reading Jeremy Narby's *Intelligence in Nature,* I mentioned to him that the strawberries that he had been meticulously tending for the past month were ready to pick. I warned him that if he were to beat the birds to them, he needed to pick them right away. Discounting, at least at the subconscious level, the birds' intelligence, he ignored my comment. Well, the birds ate the berries that afternoon. It's funny how the Western psyche, even among conscious thinkers, has a tendency to devalue experience as a legitimate way of knowing.

When Kealey later asked me how I knew that the birds were on their way to eat those berries, he assumed that my answer would include something about having read it in a book, written by a credentialed authority. When my answer was, "Oh, through observation," I noticed his eyebrows raise ever so little, even though he knew that observation was the first principle of permaculture. In all of those

First experiments in freedom: living the Good Life in rural Vermont in the 1970s. From left to right: Charlie, Pher, Sherry, and Jec.

years on the farm, I had observed enough years of birds eating ripe strawberries that there was a part of me that *was* a bird. I could feel the strawberry in my beak. I knew that this was the day it would be eaten. *Das Man* wouldn't have known that and wouldn't have believed it, even if told.

I'd been peeling an onion—myself—for thirty-five years. Onions grow in darkness, in the dirt, and when you peel them you cry. Every layer that has come off of my psychological onion has revealed another one. Watching birds eat strawberries, planting and watering seedlings, and raising livestock had slowly, tediously, peeled away

Living the Good Life today, in Mount Shasta, California, with friends.

layer after layer, moving me incrementally closer to the core—a sense of my own Being (*Sinn des Seins*).[2]

Even if my sense of who I was still contained some ambiguity, I had at least gotten out of my own way enough to know who I was *not*. I was not the final product of the dominant culture. I had been climbing out of the pit of conditioned enculturation. My existential predicament had been the rope by which I had begun to get a grip on my own being. Years of studying philosophy had created a passion for seeking the Good Life. Moving to the farm had been the first step. But what came next? What *was* the Good Life? And what were the nuts and bolts involved in living a truly Good Life?

The Good Life versus the American Dream

I had moved to Vermont during the era when America began to define itself according to its gross national product, suburban sprawl, and consensus ideology. A psychological reality of personal powerlessness and passivity—a reality tainted by conformity and complacency—was beginning to proliferate. The revolution of the sixties hadn't worked. We had been arrested, ridiculed, and marginalized.

Young people who had marched, idealistically, in the streets—advocating for racial and sexual equality, the end of war, and a return to nature—were yielding to paradigm expectations by taking corporate jobs, buying suburban homes, and joining the gym. Denim got traded for Brooks Brothers, Volkswagen buses were replaced by SUVs, and community barter got lost in the shuffle of individual 401(k)s.

Society lauded working long hours at fast-track jobs, winning, perfectionism, spending a lot of money, and accruing debt. Shopping was no longer utilitarian; it became a recreational activity. "Where's the beef?" was the mantra and, over time, yuppie parents even became complacent enough to buy their privately schooled children Barbie dolls made by exploited workers in third world countries. Wildcrafting and fair trade were still pretty far out on the horizon.

My son said that I had given him the greatest gift that anyone could ever be given. I hadn't given him any money, nor bought him a house, nor even helped him finance his first car. But I had given him freedom. I had let him make his own choices, live with the consequences of his actions, and pursue a lifestyle that best expressed his true nature. Life on the farm had taught me that I was compelled to act freely; that there was no way to avoid being free.

In Sartre's own words, I was "condemned to be free."[3] Since my initiative in being there was discovering my own authenticity, I certainly didn't want to fall prey to Sartre's concept of *bad faith*[4] by denying my total freedom, behaving like an inert object of my cultural conditioning. In Sartre's view, much of human life is a struggle to avoid the awesome opportunity of freedom. Our *bad faith* causes us to simply accept our conditioning—our enculturation—instead of making critical choices about our lives and accepting the full responsibility of the actions that result from those choices. Why?

The Consumer Paradigm

Enter "paradigms." A *paradigm* is a map of reality—a worldview, life perspective, philosophy, or mental model. It's powerful stuff. Our paradigm is the blueprint we use to build our world.[5] Paradigms usually begin with a model that weaves together ideas that make better sense than anything else. When a paradigm is working, it feels so comfortable we forget it is there: it becomes functionally invisible. We keep stride with the paradigm's framework and we conform. At some point, we have to find ways to fit into the norm, whether it's sustainable or not. We are considered healthy if we adjust to the paradigm's expectations, regardless of whether or not they actually work.

The paradigm, however, reaches a crisis, at which point it doesn't work anymore. It's not sustainable. It doesn't solve problems the way it once did. Anomalies start accumulating. The more a paradigm fails to do its job, the more we try to make it work. The paradigm needs revisioning, but because we have even forgotten that we have a paradigm, we conclude, instead, that our world is falling apart.

Sometime just after World War II, the United States experienced a consumer boom unparalleled in history. New families filled increasingly larger new homes as the baby boom began. Each family needed lots of new appliances, furniture, power tools, and cars. Americans were eager to demonstrate their new prosperity by buying lots of "stuff." Big careers, big cars, big houses, and big debt. Almost overnight, the paradigm of "more," "me," and mass consumption—the consumer paradigm, also known as the American Dream—was up and running.

2008: The Paradigm in Crisis

I was in London when the markets crashed. It was a warm autumn day in 2008 when I came up out of the subway and saw a barker on the street corner selling papers. The front-page headline, in huge print, announced that is was Black Friday. More than a little bit curious, I bought a paper and reeled at the news. It was the beginning of what we now refer to as the Great Recession. The American stock market had taken a nosedive that triggered similar responses in the global markets.

The paradigm had reached a crisis point and was no longer working. I remember wondering what would come next. And what came next were announcements of bank failures, major corporate closures, the automakers' crises, home foreclosures, layoffs and furloughs. The anomalies were accumulating. Concerns about the economy, without a doubt, dominated the 2008 U.S. election, and since Obama's victory, all eyes have been on his strategies for dealing with the failing American economy.

People were frightened. Were their jobs secure? Would they lose their homes? Could they subsist if their hours were cut or they were put on furlough? And because they had forgotten that they had a paradigm, they concluded that their world was falling apart. I didn't feel that way. I felt, instead, that we were being offered an opportunity to take a long, hard look at a paradigm that was in desperate need of revisioning. My lifestyle, which had always seemed a bit atavistic, suddenly seemed like it was light years ahead of its time. Had I, so many years ago, actually stepped backwards into the future?

Freedom from the Paradigm

While my peers had been climbing career ladders and funding their IRAs, I had contemplated what it meant to live the Good Life while pulling weeds on an organic commune. Moving to the farm in Vermont had been my first step toward what Sartre considered freedom. But, it also turned out, at a very practical level, to be freedom from an unsustainable paradigm and a shattered American Dream. Little by little, through engaged experience, I had forged my own vision of the Good Life and discovered ways to live it.

As the American economy continued to crumble in the months following the 2008 crash, I became aware that it really hadn't affected my own lifestyle. I had crafted a sustainable Good Life—although, until very recently, most of my peers had viewed it as rather eccentric. Maybe it is the part of me that waxes philosophical, but I just hadn't been able to reconcile run-away personal consumerism and creating a super-sized eco-footprint with happiness.

A report recently released by the New Economics Foundation agrees. Their survey, which looked at 143 countries, ranked the United States 114th in terms of cultural contentment and personal happiness, due to its hefty mass consumption and massive ecological footprint. According to the report, the United States was happier—and greener—twenty years ago than it is today.

Confusing Wealth with "Stuff"

I'm sure that there are still Americans who are scratching their heads and wondering how Latin American nations landed nine of the top ten spots in the survey—or how the Dominican Republic, Jamaica, Guatemala, and Vietnam all ranked above America. One of my colleagues, when presented with these results, exclaimed, "But how can that be? Those countries are all *poor!*" But are they? Doesn't it really come down to what constitutes "wealth"? Isn't "wealth" contingent upon what is considered "valuable"? If, for example, health were considered valuable, then the "wealthy" would be those who lived in ways that promoted and protected their health, as well as that of others. Behaviors such as conscious eating, moderate exercise, stress reduction, and getting sufficient sleep would all be considered critical to living the Good Life. Similarly, if education were considered valuable, then scholars would be the most "wealthy." Books, lectures, informed dialogue, and research would be part and parcel of the Good Life.

But wait a minute. Up until the market crashed in 2008, the mainstream American mindset rarely gave a second thought to what constituted the Good Life. It was pretty simple. A fast-paced "he who dies with the most toys wins" attitude meant that you were on point. Same old American Dream. Crunching time in fast forward, with a lot of labor-saving devices and appliances, mobile technology, and a ready supply of prepackaged convenience foods was the norm. So were big screen TVs, suburban housing, SUVs, and designer jeans. "Stuff" was valuable, so "wealth" meant the accumulation of "stuff" and lots of it. It would be fair to say that the emphasis was on the "goods life" instead of the Good Life.

We didn't have a lot of "stuff" on the farm. That was the point. Time stood still in Vermont, and it wasn't a place where the inhabitants rushed out to buy every new widget that came down the pike. Most towns didn't even have paved roads. Our town had a one-room schoolhouse and our post office was in the back of the general store.

The Vermont sense of rugged individualism was reinforced by a "live and let live" attitude. As long as you didn't infringe upon the rights or property of others, nobody really cared what you did or how you did it.

Things were pretty open-ended and there was plenty of room for individual expression. It was the perfect place to explore paradigms and try to define the parameters of a truly Good Life. Farmers repaired their fences with old, rusty nails they had rehammered until they were serviceable again, and their wives darned the family's winter socks with wool they had hand carded from the barnyard sheep. The Vermont paradigm, totally out of step with that of the rest of the United States, was sustainable. And it was here, by the school of hard knocks, that I began discovering the Good Life.

A Dozen Things You Can Do

- Take a good hard look at your lifestyle. Was it one that you consciously *chose?* Or, did you just create a lifestyle that emulated
societal expectations? Did your lifestyle just sort of spring up in
response to external conditions or did you proactively build a life
that was congruent with internal sensitivities?

- Equip a sturdy bicycle with panniers to use, instead of driving your
car, for jaunts into town to run errands. Keep a pair of scissors in
your bike basket for wildcrafting along your route.

- Cut and air dry wild herbs for winter tea making: get started
with rose hip, lavender, clover, peppermint, spearmint, bergamot,
raspberry leaf, strawberry leaf, and spruce bud. These teas are
not only tasty, but are beautiful, and make terrific holiday gifts
for family and friends.

- Reactivate your childhood enchantment with nature by taking
time to walk in the woods, sit by the side of a mountain stream,
or hike to a remote waterfall.

- When shopping for a home, consider a fixer-upper. This gives you
an opportunity to save money by doing renovations yourself, as
well as creating a space that expresses your uniqueness. You will
also have the option to include more environmentally friendly
materials in your living space.

- Turn your thermometer down and accessorize with cute indoor-
wear scarves, mufflers, hats, socks, and sweaters during the winter.
Make wearing long johns a habit and chose outfits that allow
you to dress in layers.

- Make a policy of having stimulating, meaningful conversation
during your family dinnertimes. Pick a topic of mutual interest
and ask everyone to come to the table prepared to have something
to say about it.

- Get rid of your TV (or at least turn it off!).

- Walk through your home and do a hard assessment of its contents.
What is "stuff" versus what items do you really need? Do you

own things that you never, or rarely, use? Could you give them
away to others who might use them?

- Repair your clothing. Sew on buttons, mend hems and seams,
  patch small tears.
- Learn to do your own home repairs. There is a lot of how-to
  information available on Internet wikis about doing minor home
  repairs.
- Make mulling spices by sun drying your orange peels and crum-
  bling the hard, dried peels together with maple sugar and spices.
  This mix is especially delicious for mulling red wines.

2

First Experiments in Freedom

*In life, a man commits himself, draws his own
portrait, and there is nothing but that portrait.*

—Jean-Paul Sartre

We had just finished a sumptuous Thanksgiving meal at the Hermitage where the conversation had been on the 2008 election and, of course, the U.S. economy. The long, wooden dining table groaned under a generous array of all raw, organic, vegan entrees. Everything that we had just eaten had been grown in our gardens, wildcrafted or bartered. The season's first yule logs were ablaze from the woodpile we had hand cut, split, and stacked on our property. The centerpiece of dried lavenders had been gathered last summer, and hung from the exposed beams in the kitchen until a few days prior, offering both scent and scenery.

We all agreed that we were grateful for the abundance we shared on this holiday. We were keenly aware that many were without homes, jobs, food, and fuel this Thanksgiving Day. America was still reeling in the wake of economic collapse. As 2008 was winding down, we wondered what lay ahead for the country. We were beginning to contemplate what a postconsumer American society might look like. Suddenly, my daughter began chuckling softly. To our questioning looks, she replied, "Oh, these napkins, I remember this fabric." Inspecting the tiny cloth napkins carefully, she asked, "Aren't these made from cloth that was in one of your old skirts, Mom?" "Well, of course," I replied.

It had been a rule, back on the farm, that everything be reused until it was, literally, compost. Old clothing, when too worn to wear, became napkins, curtains, placemats, or braided rugs. For the benefit of those guests at the table who were new to our circle of family and friends, Jec went on to explain. "I was raised on a back-to-the-earth commune in Vermont. It was a pretty unique lifestyle and it shaped the way I view the world to this very day. In fact, with the current turn of economic events in this country, I think that the way I was raised makes a lot of sense." The curiosity of some of our dinner guests mixed with the memories of others as Jec recalled those early Thanksgivings on the farm.

Thanksgiving on the farm was a big deal. Nothing—literally nothing—went on the table that had not been raised on the farm. Our first experiment in freedom involved raising all of our own food. Our master goal was to attain all-around sustainability but, after several years of trial and error, we had at least learned how to become self-sufficient with regards to food. Thanksgivings on the farm were celebrations of our having learned how to grow, preserve, and prepare all of our own food. Even though every meal, every day, was entirely made up of our own products, Thanksgiving was the grand feast that showcased our season's harvest. Our garden yielded up every sort of vegetable imaginable.

From Field to Fork

Since the Vermont growing season was short, we had learned to start seedlings in low, flat cold frames made by reusing old windows and cinder bricks. We constructed little portable roofs to place over them when a late spring snow was forecast and, more than once, shoveled them out after a big dump. Once the threat of frost was reasonably over—because in Vermont, you can never be sure!—the seedlings were transplanted into our spacious, sunny gardens.

Even though Vermont has excellent quality soils, we further enhanced it with our "black gold"—composted manure, fruit and vegetable scraps, maple leaves, grass clippings, and livestock bedding. I taught dressage professionally, and we always had no less than thirty-five horses in residence on the farm. Compost, therefore, was easy to come by—and ours was akin to rocket fuel for plants. We started in the fall, by tilling in loads of the "gold" so that it could do its magic under the snow all winter. In the spring, we tilled again and infused the newly broken soil with earthworms and mushroom spores.

Earthworms are miracle critters. A typical quarter-acre garden can host as many as 125,000 earthworms, unless the land has had synthetic fertilizers, herbicides, or insecticides used on it, which makes the soil too toxic for them to survive. Although Vermont was considerably more environmental than its neighboring states, there was no certainty that our soils hadn't been tainted by previous landowners. We, therefore, assumed a very barracuda stance about creating a certified organic land-base. Earthworms (*Lumbricus Rubellu*) aerated our soil, constantly tilling it and making it more pliable and light, providing channels for easy and deep root growth. This continuous aeration of the soil resulted in less evaporation and surface runoff, and provided for more efficient use of moisture introduced to the soil. As if that wasn't enough, the earthworms' intricate digestive tract allowed them to excrete highly nutritious fertilizer known as castings. Castings are water soluble and were immediately available to our fledgling plants. Unlike other forms of fertilizer, castings do not heat up and don't burn plants, regardless of the quantity made available to the plant.

Our new paradigm, and environmental values, though, played bumper cars with those of our squeaky clean, plastic packaged relatives who came to visit from time to time. I remember one time when my children very proudly presented my mother with a massive, wiggling earthworm dangling from the tines of a wooden rake. She freaked!

From her point of view, it was a "pest" that needed to be exterminated, announcing in no uncertain terms that we should not allow our children to touch it. In her world, it was a dirty, slimy, repulsive vermin that should be eradicated from the face of the earth. My children, on the other hand, saw earthworms as miniature gardeners.

Even my few relatives who got to the point where they could wrap their minds around my children having earthworms for playmates hit a wall when my son announced that he "remembered having been a fungus in a past life." Fungi play a critical role in natural ecosystems, and Pher, as a tiny child, seemed to have a heightened awareness of how they recycled nutrients by breaking down dead plant material. Under toddler Pher's watchful eye, we inseminated our compost with mushroom spores and created a mycological web that supported a symbiotic interrelationship between our plants and the fungi.

The children on the farm loved worms, mushrooms, and soil. When they bit into a cucumber, it was as if all of Nature had grown it for them. They had watched Her do it. She hadn't exploited others, nor had She used sweatshops. Neon colored plastic toys—manufactured for profit at the expense of others—didn't even come up on the radar of children raised on the farm. Planned obsolescence wasn't a concept that registered with them, since Nature was constantly renewing our resources. When we ate a cucumber, She ripened another.

We planted the vegetables that preferred more shade and better drainage in the sloped terraces in front of the indoor riding arena. Vermont is like a rainforest and, what it lacks in growing season length, is made up for in quality. Moderate temperatures, frequent rain, and our rich soil got us off to a good start. In no time at all the garden would be lush and green with all kinds of produce peeking out from beneath the foliage. We also grew apples, plums, pears, and cherries in a little orchard behind the barn.

Raspberry Currency

The harvest got turned into jellies and jams and there was always a colorful collage of fruit preserves, in tiny quilted glass jars, lining the old stone walls in the basement. Since we maintained several acres of cultivated raspberries, there was always enough to open the patch to neighbors in exchange for whatever they had in excess. Raspberries traded well, too, for firewood, horse-shoeing, roof repair, or any number of other goods and services.

One year, when my son was seriously injured, since our part-time jobs did not offer health insurance, we traded raspberry pies for his medical care. The doctor's family was crazy about home-baked berry pies and absolutely nobody in the valley could bake a better one than my husband, Charlie. We filled their freezer with enough pies to last their large family for a year. It was a good trade: the doctor took care of our son's body and we took care of his soul.

Barter is a viable system when financial resources are in short supply, unstable, or devalued by hyperinflation. It also offers a bridge between grassroots health care and need for the 44 million Americans, 18 percent of the population, currently without health care insurance.

Local Food

Since we didn't eat anything that we didn't grow, we didn't have things like bananas, pineapples, oranges, or mangos. From time to time, people mentioned to us that this seemed like a sort of deprivation. To us, it just seemed sensible. Although the word wasn't coined until years later, we were early *locavores. Locavores* only eat food grown locally or, in our case, on our property. Given the impossibility of identifying the pesticides used and the route taken to grow and transport, for example, a banana from Central America to our local supermarket, eating our own farm-grown produce made a lot of sense to us. We did not have to be concerned with packaging, shipping, or shelf-life and could, instead, grow and harvest crops to ensure peak qualities of freshness, nutrition, and taste. We ate seasonally, a practice that we considered to be in tune with nature.

Rich Pirog of the Leopold Center for Sustainable Agriculture reports that the average food item on the American dinner table travels 1,500 miles from the field to the fork. These products are no longer fresh, are hyperpackaged, ultrarefrigerated, and have contributed a huge carbon footprint in fuel use. Farmers receive an average of only twenty cents of each food dollar spent, and the rest of the cost goes for fossil fuel transportation, processing, packaging, refrigeration, and marketing. This definitely wasn't an economic structure with which we were comfortable.

Eatonomics

Food and economics are intimately related. The typical family spends between 15 and 20 percent of their overall household budget for food. Much of this money is not spent supporting local economies, but goes into global corporate food chains that destroy local culture and economies by being more concerned with their bottom line than they are with people or planet. In *The End of Food,* Paul Roberts writes that in the 1950s, farmers received about half the retail price for the finished food product. By 2000, the farm share had fallen below 20 percent. Cornell University sociology professor Philip Mc-Michael reports that by the mid-1990s, 80 percent of farm subsidies in Western countries went to the largest 20 percent of corporate farms, rendering small farmers increasingly vulnerable to the global market for agricultural products.

Eric Schlosser, author of *Fast Food Nation,* notes that, on any given day, one out of four Americans opts for a quick and cheap meal at a fast-food global corporate chain, without even considering that they have traded convenience for health, landscape, values, or sustainable economy. The numbers get worse: more than half of the American population eats fast food at global corporate chains at least once a week and 92 percent eat at them every month.

The World Trade Organization's guidelines regulating government subsidies enables global food corporations such as Pepsico, Kraft, Mars, Coca-Cola, McDonald's, Burger King, and Walmart to source their ingredients globally, giving them the power to force down prices, which drives more and more farmers off the land. Then these corporate giants turn around and manufacture high-profit products that seem like an unbelievable bargain to consumers.

Last year, for example, in the wake of the economic meltdown,

Kentucky Fried Chicken launched the "10 Dollar Challenge," inviting families to try to recreate a meal of seven pieces of fried chicken, four biscuits, and a side dish for less than its asking price of 10 bucks. Of course this is a virtually impossible feat, apart from dumpster diving. It doesn't take a huge leap of intellect to figure out that the KFC product might not be using the highest quality, freshest ingredients.

Urine Mindfulness

These kinds of promotional offers, already beginning to show up in the mid-1970s, frankly, scared us. Our first experiments in freedom, therefore, included growing our own produce and finding innovative ways to promote trading, barter, and exchange systems that were aligned with ecologically sound patterns and boundaries. This naturally led toward methods of zero-waste food production that cared for the earth and its inhabitants and allowed us to distribute our surplus to others in fair and equitable ways. We were stumbling our way into permaculture.

Permaculture principles are derived from observing nature. We saw things happening in the natural ecosystem that we wanted to copy. We saw the natural ecosystem as inherently sustainable if we could get out of its way. The first principle of permaculture is observation. So we observed Nature and tried to mimic Her.

The closer we got to the Earth, the more we discovered that some of the lines were pretty blurred between being a downright bumpkin and being a sustainability advocate. This became obvious to me one day when I was squatting over, and urinating into, a bucket on the backporch. At a superficial level, the behavior was the same regardless of who was doing it. The intention, though, was quite different. This always gave me cause to reflect on how seemingly identical actions could spring from radically different motivations. The folks down the road used an outhouse because they hadn't gotten around to installing indoor plumbing and a septic system. We used an outhouse because we harvested urine for our organic gardens. There is nothing better to deter wildlife than the scent of human urine.

There were tons of products on the market, calling themselves fancy names like "Liquid Fence Deer & Rabbit Repellent," which retailed for over a hundred bucks a bottle. We read the labels and learned that they were urine based. We were face to face with our social conditioning. Why did we feel okay about buying a commercial product that was predominantly coyote urine, and were so squeamish about collecting our own urine for the same purpose? The commercial product came all dressed up in sophisticated packaging, with an artistic label and handy sprayer applicator. Our bucket of urine stunk and had an ugly swarm of flies around it almost all the time. But they both did the job, so why not use our urine? The urine not only did the job, but it did it without any plastic packaging, middleman marketing, advertising, transportation, or toxic additives. This method didn't take up any space at a landfill, either, after the product was used. We were just going to have to "get over it." We got comfortable, over time, carrying that bucket of urine out to the gardens every night and splashing it around the lettuce, tomatoes, and other leafy greens. It was a pretty raw form of mindfulness training.

Shaking Off Affluenza

Even though we were riding the front wave of the new paradigm and paid lip service to unity consciousness, we were struggling with "being one" with worms, fungi, and our own urine. These experiments in freedom were turning out to be harder than we thought they would be. But, as hard as they were, we began to realize that the freedom we were cultivating wasn't just existential. We were definitely differentiating—radical individuation—but we also noticed that we were shaking off the constraints of consumer consciousness.

Dinner menus didn't require a stop at the grocery store, garden supplies didn't come in plastic bags and bottles, and we had found a way to secure health care that wasn't out of pocket. We were becoming much less dependent upon national economic trends and market vacillations. We also found ourselves able to reduce the number of hours needed spent working at jobs in town each week, allowing us more time to devote to creating a more sustainable Good Life.

Das Man, though, is a curious creature. Expose him to enough repetitions of any social concept and he'll believe it. Over time, he'll probably even think that it's his own idea. In the mid-1970s *das Man* believed that success was synonymous with a high-powered, prestigious job and doing a lot of discretionary spending—the boomers were up and running and the Age of Affluenza was dawning.[1]

A Dozen Things You Can Do

- Prepare and plant a home vegetable garden using heirloom organic seeds and plants. Start small and increase the scale of your project as you develop your skills.
- Learn how to identify and wildcraft spring and early-summer wild edibles in your own backyard. Most people's yards have sufficient wild edibles growing in them to supply a robust daily salad. In order to do this, of course, you must not spray any chemical toxins (that is, weed killers) on your lawn and adjoining areas.
- Use the fabric from old, worn-out clothing to make small, colorful table napkins. These are soft and absorbent and are really pretty when folded into tiny triangles and kept in small baskets on the table. By using the cloth napkins regularly, you save hundreds of paper towels and napkins a year.
- Air dry tall, brightly colored wildflowers until they are stiff enough to use in holiday centerpieces and other dried floral arrangements.
- Develop a compost system for your household. Start with a simple method that can evolve into a more complex system as your composting skills grow.
- Make a personal worm farm. Worm farming is a simple way of turning vegetable and fruit scraps into great soil. It can be done year round by apartment dwellers and home owners. Worm farming is particularly useful for people who would like to compost their food scraps but don't have space for a backyard compost bin.
- Enter into barter arrangements with friends, agreeing to trade goods and services that are mutually beneficial. An older person might, for example, offer to babysit a young neighbor's infant in exchange for help with shoveling snow. Or you might trade a basket of baked goods for some vegetable-starts for your garden.
- Make a real commitment to local, organic food. Buy directly from producers at farmer's markets to support local independent

agriculture. Join a local food coop. Make it a policy to not buy any food that has been transported long distances.

- Decrease the amount of packaging you buy. Use your own cloth shopping bags. Buy bulk products and put them in your own glass jars, bottles, and tins. Really scrutinize the amount of packaging that a product uses before purchasing and try to opt for those with less.
- Stop eating at fast-food restaurants that put profits into the hands of large, multinational agribusinesses.
- Habituate yourself to think about how you will dispose of something at the time you are considering buying it. If you find yourself considering an item that cannot be disposed of in an environmentally responsible way, do not buy it.
- Build low, simple cold frames out of old window panes. Cold frames will allow you to get your garden started earlier in the spring, as well as plant some hardy greens for late fall harvesting.

3

The End of Time

True time is four-dimensional.

—Martin Heidegger

On the farm, our first experiments in freedom had centered around food. Now we turned our attention to time. Time isn't part of Maslow's hierarchy of needs,[1] which seemed like a fairly serious omission to us, since much of the social pathology we saw developing in the Age of Affluenza had to do with people's perceptions of, and relationship to, time. This ran deep: people weren't even taking the time to chew their food anymore. David Kessler, author of *The End of Overeating,* notes that whereas Americans, in the past, typically chewed a mouthful of food twenty-five times before it was ready to be swallowed, the average American now chews only ten times. People were becoming more and more stuck in the stress of excess, including possession overload and time famine. They were choosing "stuff" over time.

Glossy, multicolored advertisements for sleep products graced the pages of most major magazines. People were wired and they just weren't sleeping like their grandparents had. There were even some who claimed that sleep was a "waste of time" since it didn't net any financial returns. And boomers were eating a lot of prepackaged and take-out foods because they didn't have time to prepare food at home anymore. In 1900, the typical American woman spent six hours a day in food prep and cleanup. By last year, Americans on average took thirty-one minutes a day. For many, "cooking time" consists of opening up take-out containers, dumping the contents on a plate, and throwing away the trash. All of a sudden, time was money.

Being and Time

Heidegger explored the meaning of being as defined by time. He thought that an analysis of time gave us insight into our nature, our being. Was something as important as our nature, our very being, defined by money? Was the Good Life measurable in dollars and cents? We noticed that when we met people in town and greeted them by asking, "Hey, how are you?," the reply would often be, "Busy," as they dashed past us at warp speed. The reply of "Fine, and you?," and the personal connection that accompanied it, seemed to be a pleasantry of days gone by. The pace of life had accelerated to the point where people were stretched beyond their limits with no margin, no room in their lives for rest, relaxation, and reflection. There was no space between their load and their limit, and it was becoming a source of pain and dysfunction in people's lives.[2]

Headaches, low back pain, hyperacidity, depression, anxiety, sleeplessness, and irritability got medicated with magic bullets bought over the counter. The fix was supposed to be quick and it was assumed to be "out there" somewhere. People were becoming increasingly more exteriorized as they sought a loci of control outside of themselves. Interiority takes time. Reflection and contemplation move slowly. The subjective self can't be forced to blossom.

As Karen Horney wrote, "When people wonder why success has failed to make them feel any less insecure, they only show their psychological ignorance, but the fact that they do so indicates the extent to which success and prestige are commonly regarded as yardsticks."[3] Situations and relationships began to be looked at from the standpoint of "What can I get out of this?," whether it had to do with money, prestige, contacts or ideas. The American yuppie was trading their soul for their roles.

Americans spent more on shoes, jewelry, and watches than on higher education. They spent as much on auto maintenance as on local community well-being. Nearly 30 percent of Americans bought Christmas presents for their pets while only 11 percent bought gifts for their neighbors. The scales even tipped to where America had more shopping centers than high schools.[4]

Even though the average American was complaining about unprecedented levels of busyness in everyday life and was worried about frenetic schedules and hurried children, nothing changed. After all, they were living the American Dream. Couples had no time together, families rarely ate meals together, and an onslaught of "hidden work" from proliferating emails, junk mail, and telemarketing calls dominated their lives. The average American, swept up in The Dream, worked nearly nine full weeks longer per year than his or her European counterparts. Working Americans averaged a little over two weeks of vacation per year, while Europeans averaged five to six weeks.[5]

The new consumerism had begun to jeopardize the Good Life. Getting a bargain, garage sales, and credit cards were changing the emphasis from a Good Life to a "goods life."

Life Energy and Time

While mainstream Americans were shopping on their lunch hours, patronizing outlet malls on vacation, and eventually impulse buying with a late-night click of the mouse, we were marching to a different drum on the farm. Having found ways to cut down on the number of hours that we needed to spend working at jobs in town each week, we were eager to continue experimenting with reducing our consumer-identification. We felt that Americans had been manipulated into participating in an artificial consumer culture, which yielded few true human satisfactions. We began to assess our relationship to time by asking ourselves whether or not we were receiving fulfillment, satisfaction, and value in proportion to the life energy that we spent. Was our expenditure of life energy in alignment with our values and life purpose?

University of Pennsylvania positive psychologist Dr. Martin E. P. Seligman's research indicates that satisfying work, avoiding negative events and emotions, having a rich social network, gratitude, forgiveness, and optimism are what make people happy. Seligman sees the Good Life as one in which you use your signature strengths—what you are good at—to achieve gratification in the main areas of your life. In other words, work is done for its own sake instead of for the material benefits that it brings. This sure poked a hole in the time is money concept. Suddenly, we understood clearly that time was something to be used for aligning our life energy with fulfillment, satisfaction, and value.

I had some expensive credentials hanging after my name. Normatively, I should have been single-mindedly pursuing a tenure-track appointment. But that didn't feel like my signature strength. I was good at teaching philosophy—and I was also good at teaching dressage. But I was also good at working close to the Earth—in the gardens, barns, woods, and meadows. An afternoon of gathering wild herbs and hanging them to dry in our big airy woodshed made my heart sing. And there was something about a steaming pail of fresh milk that made me feel that all was well with the world. There was a direct connection between my needs and time. If I needed lunch, I went out to the garden and got my groceries from the ground. If we needed more yogurt, we took the milking stool and went to the barn to get the milk to make it. There was a direct correlation between what was needed and the activity required to get it. We referred to this as the *work-to-goods ratio*.

1976: Work-to-Goods Ratio

We kept a lot of livestock in those days. We had thirty-six horses on the farm, as well as dairy cows, pigs, and chickens. We used a lot of hay. We made some of it on our one-hundred-and-fifty acres, mowing, tethering, and baling with horse-drawn equipment. All of my dressage horses did double-duty in the field, gardens, or woodlot, and were as comfortable hooked to a wagon as they were under saddle. Even with the thousands of bales that we produced, we still wouldn't have enough to make it through a Vermont winter.

Vermont is environmentally proactive and doesn't use chemical pesticides or weed killers along the roadways. Several times a year, they mow the roadsides and leave the lush, heavy grasses to be picked up by anyone who wants them. We got some great tans out there along those roadsides with hay rakes and forks, as load after load of fragrant, dried grasses made their way back to our hay barns. Now, it could be argued that this took a lot more time than simply buying the same amount of hay from a commercial grower. I'm not sure.

Let's look a look at the economics involved in this activity and get a sense for whether or not the work-to-goods ratio worked. Hay, in those days, cost about $80 a ton, delivered. You had to stack it in the barn yourself. We could generally put in a ton of roadside hay in about an hour, if there were four or five or us working on it. Minimum wage was $2.65 in 1978. If all five of us worked at part time jobs in order to pay for a ton of hay, we would each have had to work a little over six hours, instead of the one hour that we each worked hands-on in putting up the roadside hay. Plus, if we had bought the hay from a commercial grower, we wouldn't have gotten the tans, enjoyed the iced herbal teas or the camaraderie.

2010: Work-to-Goods Ratio

The only animals that I keep these days are horses. But I still feed them hand-harvested grasses instead of commercial hay. Every day I take a wheelbarrow and hand scythe to a neighboring alpine meadow and cut huge piles of fresh grasses for my horses. It's the best part of my day. The meadow is alive with life—butterflies, birds, geese, and deer. When I first started going to the meadow, the wildlife would run away from me. My energies were obviously incoherent. I consciously worked on staying very still, being very, very present. As I learned to stay centered in stillness, they quietly accepted my presence. I am one of them, just coming to get food from its natural setting. The sun beats down on the back of my neck as I stoop over to cut the grasses and I feel as if I am being infused with light.

The more things change, the more they stay the same. We became raw food vegans when we moved from Vermont to California. One afternoon when Kealey mentioned that he needed a large bunch of mint to put in his recipe for the evening meal, I hopped on my bicycle and went a couple of miles down the road to a large pond, where both peppermint and spearmint grow abundantly along the south shores. Within a few minutes, I had filled my bike basket and was peddling back home, enjoying the fragrance of fresh cut mints.

My more conventional neighbors routinely ask me, "How do you find the time to do these things?" Let's take a look at this, though, for a minute. I can bicycle eight miles per hour even on a bad day. That puts my transportation time at roughly fifteen minutes. The actual wildcrafting takes about ten minutes, including the time spent watching some ducklings learning to bob for fish, bringing my total time investment to about twenty-five minutes. This is roughly ten minutes less than it would be to drive into town and go to the market. There are no hidden time costs such as parking, waiting in a checkout line, or having to go to a second store because the first one didn't have it. My mints were super fresh, didn't require any packaging or gasoline use, and didn't create any auto emissions. I got some exercise, fresh air, and enjoyed the solitude at the pond.

People have been conditioned by for-profit corporate interests to think that they don't have time to create a more direct work-to-goods ratio when, in fact, it doesn't take any more time than habituated, unexamined patterns of mass enculturation.

Time Famine

The farm was a working commune, so people came and went. I remember one young man who came to live at the farm for a while who found our work-to-goods ratio concept particularly distasteful. He said that he felt out of control—like our lives were too "hand to mouth." He hated mowing the front lawn and reminded us often that we could probably get someone to "come in and do it" for very little money. He felt as if his time were worth more than what we could get the lawn mowed for by someone else.

The idea that "my time is worth more than your time" is at the very heart of so much of our social inequality. Isn't this how we justify having sweatshops in third world nations? And isn't it what holds unspoken class systems in place where, for example, being a lawyer is more important than being a landscaper? And being a CEO of a major automobile manufacturer is more important, even if the company goes bankrupt, than the workers who actually build the cars? Like it or not, it's this kind of thinking that lets us turn a blind eye toward the exploitation of peoples, social, racial, gender and ethnic discrimination, and professional prejudice.

We all get twenty-four hours in a day. Since we all get the same amount of it, how can my time be worth more than your time? Elitist ideas that equate time with money promote erroneous, unsustainable core beliefs that hold old, outworn paradigm structures in place.

So why are people in the most technologically advanced civilization in the world starved for time? One of the hooks that keep people locked into the consumer culture is the lure of convenience. We are told that convenience frees up time. This looks good on paper, but when inspected more closely, it doesn't quite ring true. Convenience does, superficially, create more time. But those conveniences are expensive and, in the long run, require people to work more hours to make more income to pay for them. In other words, people end up working more hours—thereby having less available time—to make enough money to pay for convenience. The final product of convenience is time famine. There's something wrong with this picture.

Harvard economist Juliet Schor, in *The Overworked American: The Unexpected Decline of Leisure*, argues from statistics what I had figured out from experience. According to Schor, American's work increases by one day each year. Averaging only sixteen hours of leisure a week after jobs and associated travel and communication responsibilities, working hours are longer than they were forty years ago. Bill Clinton adapted Schor's arguments to his 1992 presidential

Life at Shastao, Sherry's philosophical Hermitage.

campaign with the slogan, "Americans are working harder for less" then when Ronald Reagan was elected. Americans, essentially, spend more time *working* making money to spend on "saving time"—time that might otherwise be spent *living,* such as cooking together, enjoying lawn and garden care, or practicing arts and trades in order to serve the local community. Schor notes, though, that Americans willingly accept this time erosion in exchange for promotions, bigger salaries, and conspicuous consumption. Mass culture has replaced Good with goods.

Living on Vacation

These days I live at a philosophical Hermitage in Mount Shasta, California, where conscious travelers are invited to take refuge. The Hermitage is a continuation of the principles, and an extension of the practices, discovered on the farm in Vermont. It is committed to radical sustainability through the practice of voluntary simplicity. One of the first things that guests at the Hermitage always exclaim is how incredibly beautiful it is. Many just walk around quietly appreciating the detail that has gone into creating a truly aesthetic, welcoming space. After several days at the Hermitage, they begin to realize that the environment has been created completely in harmony with nature, and that nothing has been supplied through consumer culture.

Guests usually admit, somewhat sheepishly, that they had expected a very spartan experience—a classic misunderstanding of what is available through "voluntary simplicity." They delight in the floral bouquets, fresh from the meadow; the organic fruits and vegetables, grown here on the property in long, intensive beds; the soft, sweet-smelling sun-dried bed sheets; the way the acoustics from harpsichord, piano, harp, and recorders are carried up into the high, wooden ceilings; slow food; a library of several thousand books; the herbs hanging from the beams in the kitchen waiting to become a cup of tea; a fire in the woodstoves on chilly winter evenings with the smell of sage, grown on the slopes of Mount Shasta and hand-tied into smudge sticks, softly burning above them.

People come here because they are "on vacation." Mount Shasta is a popular vacation destination because of its natural beauty, rivers, mountains, lakes, waterfalls, swimming, canoeing, rafting, skiing, and hiking. There is no traffic and no smog. The air is fresh and the water is clean. Time slows down and people relax.

I remember one time, some years ago, when a guest and I were swimming in one of the area's pristine alpine lakes. He was childlike and kept exclaiming, over and over, as he splashed around in the water, "I am on vacation, I am on vacation!" Laying up on the shore after our swim, drying in the warm summer sun, I looked at him and, grinning, replied, " . . . and I'm not." In that moment, he got it. He realized that lifestyle was a choice. We were, in Sartre's words, "condemned to be free"—to choose. Not to choose is still a choice.

I reminded him what Heidegger had said: that we are thrust into the world, and it is up to us to find the tools to make meaning out of the chaos. He had been thrust into a world full of sports cars, triple-X-electric sex, automatic coffee pots with built-in alarm clocks, rocket ships, and escalators. He owned more than his tin-can could hold. He was making money, but, by his own admission, he wasn't finding meaning. Born in 1980, he couldn't remember a time before television, space walks, super stores, urban sprawl, Internet shopping, or any of the other accouterments of modern consumer culture. He had been raised with an assumption that meaning was to be found in profit. This was the world that he had been thrust into and in which he was expected to find meaning. It looked pretty simple: he was to find meaning in profit—except that he lived to get away from his day-to-day life and go on vacation.

Heidegger explains our being as a being-in-the-world, which means there is a relationship between the world we are in and our being. The meaning we make out of the world depends upon "the world" from which we make it. "The world" is more conceptual than it is actual. It is not homogenous. To a degree much greater than most people realize, the world from which we attempt to make meaning is actually a smorgasbord of diverse possibilities from which we can make choices. Those choices, then, appear to constitute "the world." So, we not only have the ability to create our own world, but we are actually condemned to be free to do so. The reason that more people don't do this is because mass culture has done a very good job of making them forget that this is true. People are like caged animals caught in the proverbial rat race, waiting to "go on vacation," oblivious to the fact that they could live as if they were on vacation most of the time.

Another reason that people don't visualize more sustainable and satisfying lifestyles is because they have not been introduced to realistic, appealing models. The two extremes are obvious: one being mainstream mass culture and the other being a complete retreat to the woods, often referred to as homesteading. Neither of these extremes satisfactorily reduces a person's workload to the point that they are "on vacation" most of the time.

Our experiments in freedom taught me how to adapt and implement a postconsumer lifestyle that combined my abilities to maintain rich intellectual satisfaction, active professional engagement, and abundance with simplicity. The key lies in knowing that this is a *choice*— that I have voluntarily chosen a particular lifestyle. My lifestyle isn't something that just happened. Neither am I simply a victim of my life. I made choices, in those years on the farm, that involved a desire to live in daily awareness of the consequences of each act, sought to minimize my impact on the earth through living closer to the source of life, and to reduce the processes that separated me from that source while still maintaining a strong and vital professional orientation. It wasn't an either/or decision; it was synergistic. It was a synthesis of my roles with my soul.

The Gospel of Consumption

Mass culture has been conditioned to expect someone else to make their choices for them, to tell them what to do, to be, and to think. Most people are unaware that they are consumer fundamentalists, rarely asking whether or not concepts such as limitless growth, ruthless competition, more stuff, and other "fundamentals" of today's consumer environment are even up for question. And up until the recent economic collapse, most people hadn't thought twice when they heard that, according to modern economic thinking, their primary role in society was to be a model consumer, mere functionaries in a vast economic machine for the "growth" and the accumulation of money.

Twentieth-century consumer interests have perpetuated this headset ever since public relations pioneer, and double nephew of Sigmund Freud, Edward Bernays masterminded his manipulation technique, called the "engineering of consent." Bernays maintained that entire populations were vulnerable to unconscious influence and, thus, susceptible to want things that they do not need. By linking consumer products and ideas to people's unconscious desires, he was able to manipulate consumer buying trends in a way that had never before been possible. In Bernays's own words, "If we understand the mechanism and motives of the group mind, is it not possible to control and regiment the masses according to our will without their knowing about it?"[6]

Bernays used propaganda, psychological manipulation, and celebrity endorsement to peddle his clients' wares, control the mass mind, and build an empire based on profits. Ernest Dichter, widely considered the "father of motivational research," referred to this as "the secret-*self* of the American *consumer.*" The *Century of the Self* was up and running.[7]

Even though Bernay's work created a tsunami of personal consumption, industrialists feared that the frugal habits maintained by most post-Depression American families would be difficult to break. Perhaps even more threatening was the fact that the industrial capacity for turning out goods seemed to be increasing at a pace greater than people's sense that they needed them. It was this latter concern that led Charles Kettering, director of General Motors Research, to write a 1929 magazine article entitled "Keep the Consumer Dissatisfied." Along with many of his corporate cohorts, he was defining a strategic shift for American industry—from fulfilling basic human needs to creating new ones. In other words, people had to be convinced that no matter how much they had, it wasn't enough.

President Herbert Hoover's 1929 Committee on Recent Economic Changes celebrated Kettering's conceptual breakthrough: "Economically we have a boundless field before us; that there are new wants which will make way endlessly for newer wants, as fast as they are satisfied." So instead of utilizing machines and technology to save labor and, consequently, infuse culture with more discretionary time, they were used to increase productivity—to make more "stuff" for consumers to buy. This, of course, created more time famine for people, as they had to work more in order to make more money to pay for all of this new stuff. Benjamin Kline Hunnicutt remarked that "businessmen, economists, advertisers, and politicians preached that there would never be 'enough' because the entrepreneur and industry could invent new things for advertising to sell and for people to want and work for indefinitely."[8]

A New Gospel

Life on the farm was a conscious counterresponse to what economist Edward Cowdrick called the *gospel of consumption.* We sought sustainability through cooking food, fresh from the garden, from scratch; by reducing waste, lowering consumption, composting kitchen and yard scraps, and using the least noxious technologies possible to accomplish every task. In living this way, we inevitably reduced our reliance on consumer goods and relied more on our own skills and abilities, including our imaginations and one another.

Every fall, we gathered apples from our orchards and from neighboring trees and made fresh cider. It was a time that we all looked forward to with eagerness. The children scrambled up the trees and shook the apples down while the adults put them into burlap bags and hoisted them onto the back of the pickup truck. The orchards were high on the mountain, where the air was fresh and crisp—like the fresh apples—and we enjoyed the magnificent colors of the Vermont foliage on the surrounding hills. Once back down to the farmhouse, we set up the cider press on the front porch and began our cider-making operation.

Cider making was in part utilitarian, in part a community activity, with strong aesthetic and craft components. The porch came alive with the comings and goings of those who brought in the bags of apples and those who ran the press. The activity naturally became the medium for something more important than just making cider. Stories, jokes, teasing, quarreling, practical instruction, songs, sorrows, and problems were shared. As the strong, sweet juices poured out of the hand-turned cider press, invariably someone who had stopped by would remind us that we could "make more cider faster" if we had an electric press, inferring that we would also have some to sell for a profit. Some of these well-meaning guests would even go so far as so draw sketches of how we could hook our cider press up to a generator or car battery to "save time." They didn't understand that we had consciously traded the concept of alienated work for a more complex and convivial kind of working together.

The struggle "against time" and the concept of alienated work had its roots in the early days of the Industrial Revolution when workers resisted industrial capitalism. Traditionally, work had been an integral part of community, in the same way that we worked on the farm. Workers came and went throughout the day, trading stories and gossip and generally following a leisurely pace that allowed them to do all sorts of things that were not "on task"—activities having as much to do with the ordinary details of family and community as with "the job." Bursts of concentrated work alternated with relaxed periods of socializing.

Moreover, people enjoyed considerable control over their tasks by using their signature strengths. Not only were they able to set their own schedules and control their work rhythms, they had the chance to hone traditional skills and incorporate their own creative ideas into their work. The things they produced were as much as part of the community's culture as the songs and stories, arguments and gossip, that surrounded them in the workshop. Industrialists, however, could not afford to have workers doing "other things" at work. They saw this as detrimental to the effort for which they were paying good money. For industry to be productive and capitalism to prosper, workers had to be convinced to work, and work only, when they were "on the clock" and to accept a clear separation between their work and their lives![9]

Integrating Work and Life

There was no separation between our work and our lives when sugaring season came in the Green Mountains. After a long, hard Vermont winter, we were always ready to get outside in the spring sunshine and hang the buckets for gathering sap. Maple sap flows when the temperature is below freezing at night and above it during the day. Usually this meant that there was still so much snow on the ground that we had to break through it to get into the sugar orchard.

Our old Morgan stallion loved this job! We hooked him to a sleigh, loaded with sugaring buckets and spouts, and headed down into the grove of sugar maples. He pranced and danced his way through the leftover winter snow, as happy to be out in the spring sunshine as we were. He was an incredible driving horse, and he would carefully negotiate the tight turns between the trees, and stand bolt still as the children punched through snow drifts to set out the buckets. The adults manned the hammers and drove the spouts into the trees, gleefully finding spout holes from previous years as they reminisced about how good or bad a particular season had been. After the buckets were all hung, the waiting began. Someone would go out each day and check to see if the sap had begun to run—and, finally, one day it would!

And when it began to run, it really ran. We would have to work furiously to stay ahead of it with our gathering efforts. Every day— sometimes twice a day—the old stallion was pressed into service again as we emptied the buckets, sticky with fresh maple sap, into the holding tank that he pulled in the sleigh. When the tank was three-quarters full, he would dig in and pull that load up to the sugarhouse where we boiled the sap into maple syrup. It takes roughly thirty-six gallons of sap to make a gallon of syrup, so the wood-fired arch would be burning twenty-four hours a day. We took shifts around the clock to man the evaporator, watching carefully to make sure that the sap flowed smoothly through the maze of pans and didn't scorch.

When the first batches of syrup were ready to come off, we poured it, boiling hot, onto bowls of packed snow—sugar-on-snow—which we gobbled up like kids in a candy store. The rest of the syrup was put up in glass jars, for the next year's use on the farm and to give away to our friends and neighbors. We also made maple candy, pressed into little molds and cooled, that rivaled anything you could buy in a gourmet confectionery shop.

We bragged about creating something both useful and beautiful when we entered our maple products in local fairs and festivals. We discussed the clarity and color of the syrup, the taste and texture of the candy, and the various grades that particular year's crop had yielded. Since our maple products were homemade, they had a special appeal to family and friends who agreed that their commercial counterparts were inferior in taste, appearance, and general appeal.

Handcrafted cultural goods had a special attribute in that, when we shared them with others, we did not lose them. Instead, we increased our own pleasure in them. By dividing them, we multiplied them.

Unlike commercial recreation, sugaring together was special. We shared a common purpose that gave the adults a chance to give children a glimpse of what their childhood had been like and reex-perience the smells and tastes of their heritage. The children on the farm also got hands-on experience in planning and seeing a project through, thereby learning discipline and responsibility while building self-confidence.

It was part of an embedded life—a life that was connected at every possible point with the Earth and with community. On the farm, I learned to make a *life*—one where I woke up every morning eagerly anticipating the day ahead—and not just make a *living*. A conscious, mindful approach to sustainability had pointed the way to my becoming a master of my own time—to making time four-dimensional. It was like being on vacation all the time, even though I worked—and often quite hard—every day.

A Dozen Things You Can Do

- Cultivate a habit of chewing each mouthful of food no less than twenty-five times before swallowing. Really savor the taste and texture of each bite. Stop eating before you are completely full: only eat enough to satisfy you, not to stuff you.
- Put as much energy into developing your interior life as you do into creating your exterior life. Meditate or pray, do yoga or tai chi, and read inspirational literature.
- Foster your creativity. Make art, music, poetry, or crafts. Do things just for the sake of doing them—not because they produce income or generate commodities.
- Complete an online self-rating scale to determine your individual signature strengths. Try to integrate these signature strengths into the way that you live your life.
- Calculate your work-to-goods ratio. Is it sufficiently direct? Are there places that you could make it more satisfying?
- Assess your addiction to convenience. Are you working overtime in order to make more money to spend on "time saving" appliances, equipment and services, or to buy expensive "convenience" items?
- Put up a clothesline and line dry your laundry in the fresh air and sunshine. The fresh smell of line-dried bed sheets will make your heart sing.
- Buy fresh, wholesome, organic ingredients and cook meals from scratch. Say goodbye to processed, prepackaged foods. Invite household members into the kitchen to help and enjoy the added bonus of time spent together.
- Go fall apple picking. Many local orchards offer pick-your-own Saturday afternoons. Bring home the bounty and invite friends for fresh, homemade apple pie and herbal teas.
- Sponsor work-bees that integrate work and life. If you have a big home project to do, turn it into an event. Invite friends to help, for example, repaint a back bedroom after which you all share a

potluck dinner together, complete with musical instruments.

- Handcraft cultural goods. Enjoy time spent together with a few close friends, making crafts that reflect your cultural and geographic heritage. If, for example, you live in the Sierras, find ways to incorporate massive pine cones, or smooth rocks left behind by the spring snow-melt, into craft projects.
- Set up a makeshift picnic table, complete with a beautiful tablecloth, a fresh bouquet of wildflowers, and candles, next to your vegetable garden and invite a handful of close friends over for salad and wine. Plan to gather just before twilight when the golden light is streaming. Have a tub of lukewarm water for vegetable washing and some hand towels available and let your guests "pick their own dinner" from the garden. Claude Monet was known to have dined in his gardens at Giverny.

4

Putting the Why and the How Together

He who has a why to live can bear almost any how.

—Friedrich Wilhelm Nietzsche

A man came to my philosophical Hermitage a few months ago on personal retreat. Jerry was in transition. He was a European who had, many years ago, come to America seeking his fortune—and he had met his goal. He had become a self-made millionaire—another example of the American Dream. But intimate relationships, although he longed for one, hadn't worked out for him. Neither did he have a circle of close friends with whom to share his fine home, pool, cars, and horses. I had heard other people describe him as an irritable, unpleasant, self-absorbed man. In short, his single-minded pursuit of wealth had turned him into an empty shell.

The recent economic crash, however, had changed all of that. The man who visited me was content, peaceful, and gracious. He had lost his entire fortune. After getting over the initial shock of the loss, he began to see that he was free. He had studied Buddhism for years, but confessed to not having "got it." The concepts of impermanence and nonattachment just hadn't registered. Suddenly, in the course of

a few weeks, nothing in his life was the same. He was living impermanence and had nothing to which to be attached. "What good is
a fortune if it cost me twenty years of my life," he asked one day. "I
can never get those twenty years back," he said with a sigh, "years
that I could have used finding a life-partner, maybe having children,
and even learning to paint."

As he walked around the Hermitage, appreciating the diversity
of original artwork on the walls, he continued soulfully, "I've always
wanted to paint." And then he broke into a big grin and said, "and
now I have time." I invited him to spend as much time as he wanted
to in the Hermitage's simple art studio. Like a child at play, he spent
days exploring color, line, and composition. The art studio at the
Hermitage is on the ground floor, on the backside of the house. It's
quiet and offers uninterrupted creative time. It has a door that opens
right out into the wooded horse paddocks. If time at the easel stiffened
his back, he could step into an adjoining outdoor sauna and let the
dry heat work on it. As his creative juices flowed, ideas for getting
back up on his feet financially began to come to him. He began to
see options and realize that he could make a living that didn't cost
him his life.

Stoicism and the Good Life

By the time Jerry left the Hermitage, he had formulated a fairly good
preliminary plan for getting back up on his feet while still nourishing the needs of his soul. He was crafting a blueprint for the Good
Life. Jerry's process seemed like a contemporary expression of Stoic
philosophy. More than 2,200 years have passed since the Stoics
gathered in the marketplace of Athens to discuss the Good Life. In
many ways, though, Stoicism is as relevant, as urgently *practical,* in
twenty-first-century America as it was 1,900 years ago in the Roman
Empire when Epictetus set up his school.

Epictetus's Stoic philosophy was basically that the goal of life was
to live in harmony with nature. To live the Good Life, we must both
live in accord with our human nature—as essentially rational, reflec-
tive, and thoughtful beings—and conform to the actual conditions of

the natural world. The Stoics believed that rational choices should always lead us to behave wisely, courageously, justly, and temperately. These choices—along with our attitudes, emotional responses, and mental outlook—are up to us to control.

We cannot be forced to have beliefs, form judgments, or attempt actions without consciously, voluntarily *choosing* to do so. Events in the world, on the other hand, including all the beliefs and actions of other people, are essentially not in our control. Such things as the stock market and the recent economic downturn are ultimately not up to us. In this respect, Stoicism is a kind of coping strategy.

The central idea is to try to do the right thing, in every situation, without losing one's calm, becoming frustrated, or getting angry. "Doing the right thing" includes fulfilling our responsibilities to family, friends, coworkers, neighbors, fellow travelers, fellow citizens and, in general, all human beings. It is not a survival of the fittest or dog-eat-dog philosophy.

Since we all naturally want to be happy, the Stoic way to live is to train ourselves to limit our desires and concerns to what is up to us; the other side of the equation is not to worry about, fear, or get upset by things that are not up to us. The Stoics believed that if we strive every day to do our best, then we can accept the rest. The Stoics believed that the universe is ordered by the Logos, which is the "meaning" and order of the universe. Each and every event, physical and historical, has a place within this larger context. Since the order is meaningful, nothing happens which is not part of some larger good. One essentially has only two choices in life: to accept the circumstances of one's life or to futilely resist those circumstances. Through his recent tribulation, Jerry had come to accept the circumstances in his life and, in doing so, had attuned to the Logos. He was aligned with the meaning of the universe. Profit wasn't his bottom line any longer.

The Search for Meaning

Viktor Frankl, in *Man's Search for Meaning*, wrote that "man's main concern is not to gain pleasure or to avoid pain but rather to see a meaning in his life."[1] He continues, "People have enough to live, but nothing to live for; they have the means but no meaning."² What makes a human life good—what makes it worth living and what must we do, not just merely to live, but to live well?

Each time Robert Inglehart, political scientist at University of Michigan, administers his World Values Survey, he finds that respondents express increasingly greater concern for spiritual and immaterial matters. He thinks he sees the advanced world in the midst of a gradual shift from materialist values, emphasizing economic and physical security, toward postconsumer priorities, emphasizing self-expression and the quality of life.

As for Jerry, as well as for many other people, the recent economic crisis, albeit wreaking havoc with their lives, contains an element of opportunity.

According to Gregg Easterbook, in *The Progress Paradox,* "A transition from material want to meaning want is in progress on an historically unprecedented scale—involving hundreds of millions of people—and may eventually be recognized as the principal cultural development of our age."³ Prior to the consumer craze of the past several decades, a nation's economy was a subset of its overall culture. In other words, the economy was softly nestled into a larger cultural context. As the gospel of consumption spread from sea to shining sea, however, a cultural inversion took place. Incrementally and almost insidiously, culture began to be the subset of its economy. That is, the nation became subservient to its economy.

Emphasis shifted from the pursuit of happiness to the accumulation of wealth. People were defined by their "stuff." Having a lot "stuff" indicated that one was successful. The only fly in the ointment was that people were not happy. There are currently approximately 19 million clinically depressed Americans, or 9.5 percent of the population in any given one-year period. Depression currently affects so many people that it is often referred to as the common cold of mental illness.

And it is not only adults who are affected. Wandering among suburban estates and prep schools are overlooked children of a perplexed generation. Their lives overflow with affluence, yet ironically, the facade of apparent success may hide a gloomy world of emptiness, anxiety, and anger. In *The Price of Privilege,* Madeline Levine, a clinical psychologist practicing in Marin County, California, claims that the nation's latest group of at-risk kids comes from affluent, well-educated families. Despite advantages, these children experience disproportionately high rates of clinical depression, substance abuse, anxiety, eating disorders, and self-destructive behaviors. Based on criteria from the U.S. Centers for Disease Control and Prevention, Levine says these children "are exhibiting epidemic rates of emotional problems beginning in junior high school and accelerating throughout adolescence."[4]

In 2005, the National Institute of Health reported that 40 million Americans suffer from an anxiety disorder. The data collected indicated that much of this anxiety originated in dissatisfaction toward, or downright hatred of, their work. The 2000 annual "Attitudes in the American Workplace VI" Gallup Poll, reported that 80 percent of workers feel significant, negative stress on the job, and 25 percent report having felt like screaming or shouting because of job stress. A subsequent 2000 Integra Survey indicated that 62 percent of the American workforce routinely ended the day with work-related neck pain, and 34 percent reported difficulty in sleeping because they were too stressed-out from their jobs. Over half said they often spend twelve-hour days on work-related duties and an equal number frequently skip lunch because of job demands. This trend is strongest among workers under the age of twenty-five, less than 39 percent of who are satisfied with their jobs. Workers age forty-five to fifty-four have the second lowest level of satisfaction, with over 57 percent reporting professional dissatisfaction.

For many, the workplace is a golden cage—a place they stay because of the paycheck, not because they feel adequately engaged or stimulated. American workers are forgetting how to fly. In return for a paycheck, they are loyal to work they hate, and they live for those sadly diminishing hours when they can pour themselves into activities they would much rather be doing. All the while, they try to quell the little nagging voice inside their heads that they ought to be doing what they love—that there ought to be some congruence between their *life* and making a *living*. Moreover, they can't shake the concern, no matter how deeply they try to bury it under "stuff," about not having sufficient *meaning* in their lives.

Gross National Happiness

It's there, buried under piles of consumer goods, hours of unproductive psychotherapy, and disappearing front porches—American's nagging realization that they aren't happy. Measuring cultural quality by the Gross National Product instead of—for example, like Bhutan—by the Gross National Happiness has led to lives where, too often, meaning, purpose, deep life experience, and gratitude are missing. No matter how fast we run, we can't seem to outdistance knowing that happiness delivers a bigger mental value than financial value.

In the whole tradition of Western literature, the one book that, more than any other, attempts to define *happiness* is Aristotle's *Ethics*. Basically, Aristotle taught that the requirement for happiness was "a complete life"—and a happy life was a Good Life. Aristotle believed that happiness was the ultimate good—the highest good, the supreme good. This definition, though, comes into clearer focus when we understand that Aristotle considered happiness as a state of human well-being that leaves nothing more to be desired. A happy man, Aristotle would say, is the man who has everything he really needs—not what he *wants*, but what he *needs*. He has those things that he needs to realize his full human potential. That is why Aristotle says that the happy man wants for nothing.

For Aristotle, a happy life is a mix of health, wealth, friendship, knowledge, nature, and virtue. Consider the modern American über-consumer who thinks that happiness consists primarily in accumulating "stuff." In order to make enough money to buy all of this stuff, he ruins his health, experiences personal alienation, does not take part in the vital life of his community, and is, consequently, subject to constant stress and anxiety. But there he sits: Captain Consumer, proudly ogling all of his stuff. Is he a happy man or is he miserable? Aristotle would say that he is miserable—the most tragic type of human misery. For he has stunted his human development. He has unintentionally deprived himself of most of the good things of life—health, wisdom, friendship, and meaningful human relationship—in order to acquire "stuff." He has traded the pursuit of happiness for "stuff."

Liberation Capitalism

We practiced a form of *Liberation Capitalism*, to use a term coined by Benjamin Kline Hunnicutt, on the farm. We structured a lifestyle that was intentionally designed to include time spent with one another, in community and in nature. We participated in the marketplace and we were all active in our professions, but we weren't governed by them. We had consciously chosen not to deprive ourselves of the good things of life. We learned, worked, appreciated, and played together. We did not define ourselves by how much "stuff" we had accumulated. As each of our individuation deepened, there were no "Joneses to keep up with." Our lives were so differentiated from that of the mainstream, developing consumer culture that comparison wasn't even a consideration.

The farm was like a giant rock tumbler in which we all got polished. We went into the tumbler with a lot of rough edges and, if we tumbled around enough in there together, we came out smooth and polished. Communal living has a way of eroding the ego. This was especially transparent during holiday celebrations. Since we all came from different backgrounds, we all had different holiday traditions that we considered sacrosanct. In the early years, we used to argue, sometimes quite vehemently, about how various holidays should be kept. As the tumbler turned, however, our fiestas became more and more eclectic and inclusive. While neighboring families' Christmas celebrations put their credit card balances through the roof, ours were homespun and simple. But our simplicity was neither bleak nor sparse.

Christmas on the Farm

We started preparing for Christmas a full month ahead. We opened the farm on Christmas Eve to all of our friends and families. People would start pouring in during the afternoon on Christmas Eve and the excitement built as more and more people arrived. The old black Morgan stallion was groomed and ready—eating hay in his box stall while he waited for his role—and the sleigh and harness had been polished and buffed until they glistened.

The farmhouse kitchen bustled as the holiday treats came out of the woodstove and were put on plates to sit in the warming oven until the very last minute. We grew and ground our own wheat, so we never took baked goods for granted, as we had worked hard to mill the ingredients from which they were made. The dried fruits in the cookies had been picked in our orchards the summer prior and sun dried up on the porch roofs. They were chewy little bursts of goodness that blended perfectly with our maple sugar–sweetened cookies. Hot teas mulled on the stovetop, made from the herbs that had been drying all fall in the woodsheds. Lavender, red and white clover, rose petals, and mints mixed together into a fragrant floral tea that we spiced with dried bergamot, harvested in late summer from the terraces in front of the indoor riding arena.

The children excitedly carried the little rounds of soft cheeses, made from the milk of our cows, as well as pats of farm-fresh butter and small pitchers of cream to the table. Cider, that had hardened nicely in the cellar, simmered softly on top of the wood cookstove, ready to be enjoyed. Loaves of handmade bread, baked slowly in the wood oven, were sent to the table with accompanying cheddar cheeses that had hung from the rafters in the cellar, curing since the summer past. Jars of farm-preserved pickles and relishes sat beside platters brimming over with sun-dried zucchini chips and tomatoes, and bowls of salsas that reminded us of the smell of our garden in midsummer. And, of course, there would always be plenty of tiny maple candies, molded into the shapes of maple leaves, little people and animals.

There would always be snow, and usually plenty of it. People arrived in heavy outer garments, mittens, gloves, and huge, insulated boots. As they warmed themselves by any of the three raging woodstoves in the old farmhouse, outerwear would be discarded and hung to keep warm around the stoves. The smell of wool, warming and drying, still reminds me of Christmas. The adults would begin sharing stories and swapping tales—getting one another caught up on births, deaths, and other important news from their respective families—while the children ran around the tree pointing to favorite decorations and hoping that Santa hadn't forgotten them.

We always put the tree in about a week before Christmas. We waited to go out and get it until there was enough snow in the fields to hook the younger stallion up and take him into the woods on a mission to find the perfect Christmas tree. It was good training for the young stallion. He was impatient and full of himself, and going after the tree gave him a good opportunity to learn to stand still while we examined each potential tree, discussing its relative plusses and minuses. He would sometimes paw the ground and snort, but nobody ever paid any attention to his impatience as the excitement of getting the tree always preempted his opinions. Sometimes he fussed that he was far too fancy to have to wear the work harness, but he always settled down and brought the tree proudly back to the farm. After enough years of getting the tree, a young stallion matured and earned the status of being the "old stallion," who was trusted enough to get the better jobs!

The better jobs included bringing Santa, complete with bells and a burlap bag of gifts, by sleigh right to the door of the farmhouse. We had an old Santa suit that we kept in a suitcase high up in the hay loft where the kids never found it. At least, if they did, nobody has ever told me about it! A favorite uncle, who had the belly for the job, snuck away from the Christmas Eve festivities at the house, donned the suit, and—with help from some of the other men in the group—got the old stallion ready to play the starring role.

As the sun set and darkness began to creep into the hills, the children started looking out the windows, waiting—because Santa came every year about that time. They would get as quiet as lambs, straining to hear those sleigh bells. And, sure enough, the old Morgan stallion always came trotting—head high, snapping his forelegs up in a park trot—up that dirt road toward the farmhouse. And, of course, Santa was at the reins! One of the men inside the house would always be ready, right on cue, to go out and take over on the reins, as Santa got out of the sleigh, threw the bag of gifts over his back, and strolled into the kitchen. Talk about excitement!

The bag of gifts had been prepared, sometimes as much as a month ahead, by the women in our group. We had handmade tiny dolls and stuffed animals; knitted socks and mittens; crafted bean bags and balls; sanded, stained, and polished wooden board games; and strung beads for necklaces and bracelets. We had also refurbished old toy trucks and tractors that we had found in secondhand stores in town. Carefully, stripping, sanding, and repainting them, we had given them second lives—recycled them—with a whole new crop of youngsters eager to push them around the floors and sandboxes. The gifts had been meticulously wrapped in colored newspaper, usually taken from the comic sections of the local paper, and labeled for each child so that Santa could hand them out. And since the wrappings weren't commercial paper, they could go directly into the woodstoves on Christmas morning to help kindle a new day's fire.

As the children enjoyed their new things, adults feasted on the goodies that had been so carefully prepared. After a while, the furniture was pushed back in the living room to make room to hang the piñata. The piñata had been made, late at night, after the farm children were in bed, out of homemade paper maché, using flour paste and sheets torn from newspapers and magazines. Each layer had been carefully dried, up in the attic where it was out of sight, before the next was applied. Layer after layer was applied, so that it would be very, very strong. Finally, the outer layers were shaped to form each year's animal—elephants, tigers, dinosaurs, and turtles. And finally, when it was dry and rock hard, it had been painted in bright tempura colors—festive and fun! The center was hollow and was stuffed with candies, little presents, and confetti.

Each child was given a long stick and took turns swinging at the piñata. The youngest children, who posed no real threat to the piñata, went first. They whirled and swung, missing it over and over.

As the older children were given their turn, the piñata was raised a bit higher and put into a gentle swinging motion, so that it was harder to hit. Finally, one of the older children, seasoned from years of trying, would break it and the contents came pouring to the ground. Each child would fill their pockets with treats gathered from the bounty, as well as happily share their portion of the take with parents and grandparents.

Then, piping hot from the wood oven, came the parade of pies. They were all made with farm grown and preserved berries, pumpkins, squash, and apples. The berries, picked at the height of the season, had been flash frozen and stored in one of our huge chest freezers. Pumpkins, squash, and apples had been brought in, often by the children on their wagons, and carefully stored in the root cellar. The apples had been put in bushel baskets and stacked along the walls of the root cellar, while the pumpkins and winter squash had been carefully spaced on the shelves above. The root cellar was tempting to mice and other critters, so we had to be especially mindful to always keep the airtight door firmly sealed, lest we have little nibble marks on the produce.

The pies were gobbled up several pieces at a time by the merrymakers, with steaming mugs of spiced teas and ciders. And, of course, the cows had offered up a limitless supply of milk to be frothed for the children. As people began to get their fill of pies, invariably someone would break out the musical instruments—guitars, recorders, tambourines, bells, horns, and whatever else anyone knew how to play. We would spend some time tuning up and then launch into all sorts of holiday music. We played a multicultural mix of classic Christmas carols as well as ancient Celtic solstice melodies. When we thought we were playing well, we donned coats, boots, mittens, scarves and hats, and struck out to serenade the neighboring farms.

We walked, like a tidal wave of season's cheer, from farm to farm—often with heavy snow falling—singing and playing our instruments with abandon. Strong, virile young fathers carried the children up on their shoulders, above the crowd, so that they could see everything around them. Since it was an annual event, our neighbors expected us and met us with warming cups of cocoa and more cookies.

Since our mountaintop neighborhood was tiny, with only a half-dozen farms, we would be back at our place again in time to stop by the stables and sing a merry tune or two to the horses and other livestock. Then, one of the women would step forward and share the myth about how animals could speak at midnight on Christmas Eve. The children ran attentively from animal to animal, listening. As the children hoped to hear their favorite animal speak, we busied ourselves giving every animal an extra ration of hay, so that they, too, could have a bit of a holiday feast. The animals never spoke, and no one ever noticed.

Making Memories Instead of Debt

The celebration was voluntarily simple. We made memories instead of debt. Nobody maxed out their credit card, there were no bills deferred until the first of the year. It had all come from engagement with our own lives. We weren't *making* livings, we *were* living. Our pantries were full and so was the woodshed. We had learned to live with one another in harmony. Working side by side, day after day, had worn away any sense of entitlement or being special.

It was Maslow's hierarchy in action. We grew intrinsically, each becoming more of who we were. We were moving toward self-actualization as a natural outgrowth of living our lives. This sense of deep engagement with life taught me how to create an efficient perception of reality that extended into all other areas of my life. I learned to accept myself, others, and the natural world the way they were. The support of shared community allowed old guilt and inhibitions to fall away.

Since we were unhampered by convention on the farm, I developed spontaneity in my inner life. My ethics became autonomous at the same time I had become motivated towards continual improvement. Creating our own intentional community showed me that I could choose resilience in the face of hard knocks. My sense of appreciation, moment to moment, was freshened. Choosing a lifestyle where *how* I lived was congruent with *why* I was living, brought Abraham Maslow's words into focus:

> Feelings of limitless horizons opening up to the vision, the feeling of being simultaneously more powerful and also more helpless than one ever was before, the feeling of ecstasy and wonder and awe, the loss of placement in time and space with, finally, the conviction that something extremely important and valuable had happened, so that the subject was to some extent transformed and strengthened even in his daily life by such experiences.[5]

I had begun the long walk toward self-actualization. This was, for me, the goal of living. I did not live to make money to buy stuff. I had a much bigger picture in sight: I lived to reach my full human potential. As I had begun to identify some ways to do it, my *how* and my *why* were on the same page.

A Dozen Things You Can Do

- Read aloud to one another. Chose books in which you are mutually interested and take turns reading to one another. Enjoy the stimulating discussions that are bound to ensue from the shared experience.
- Incorporate stress-reduction activities such as massage, hot-tubing, and saunas into your schedule. Treat them with the same importance that you would a dental appointment or meeting with your tax consultant. Do not skip them because you are "too busy."
- Comb the secondhand stores and thrift shops for old cookie cutters. Make homemade cookie dough and invite some friends over to bake. Rolling and cutting cookie dough, with a hot cup of wildcrafted, herbal tea in hand, will put you in touch with your inner child.
- If you live in a forested area, consider installing an environmentally friendly woodstove to supplement home heating needs. You can often find landowners willing to allow you to cut up fallen trees on their land in exchange for the cleanup.
- Save colored comics from Sunday papers and use them as gift-wrap paper.
- Instead of going out for expensive commercial amusement, invite friends in for an evening of board games. Listen to the laughter as people challenge each other's words in Scrabble or jump the gun to yell "Uno."
- Keep your eye on the Internet swap boards and try to find some old snowshoes. One size fits all and you'll have fun going outside on them even when weather is blustery.
- Consider refinishing and recycling old wooden toys, found in the attic or thrift stores, as holiday gifts for young children: old rocking horses, runner sleds, doll furniture, blocks, trains, and games can take on a second life with a bit of sanding and a fresh coat of color.

- Plan an evening of holiday caroling your neighbors. Let them know that your group is coming and be welcomed with steaming mugs of hot cocoa and platters of cookies.
- Make a homemade holiday gingerbread house with friends and family. Your first one can be a tiny chalet. In just a few years, though, you'll be creating whole villages!
- Hand sew toys for infants out of old socks and worn out clothing. Soft dolls, little stuffed animals, and hand-puppets are fun to make for tiny ones—sewing in love with every stitch!
- Declare a no-commercial-gift policy for holidays and birthdays, only exchanging gifts that are homemade. You'll be delighted with what you receive—original artwork, plants, baked goods, confectionery, crafted items, or gift certificates for a friend's help with yard work!

5

The New Stationary State

*No great improvements in the lot of mankind are possible until
a great change takes place in the fundamental constitution of
their modes of thought.*

—John Stuart Mill

I went to the farm in the mid-1970s because I was seeking meaning through learning to live a sustainable lifestyle. I realized that consumer culture was on a collision course with disaster. Human beings were, in trying to realize the American Dream, destroying the world. I wanted to work with others who were committed to gaining the technical knowledge, communication skills, and material resources to grow food, decrease their carbon footprint, assure clean air and water, and produce renewable energy. I wanted to participate in a life-sustaining community.

I felt that a mounting economic storm was fast approaching but was thirty years ahead of my time. The market crash of 2008, in conjunction with climate change, peak oil, overpopulation, and environmental pollution, began unraveling the corporate-led global economy that holds consumer culture in place and offered a dramatic restructuring of every aspect of modern life. It was the beginning of the Great Turning.[1]

The Great Turning

The Great Turning is a name for the essential adventure of our time: the opportunity to shift from the industrial growth, consumer-based society to a life-sustaining, postconsumer civilization. The ecological and social crises we face are inflamed by an economic system dependent on accelerating growth. Economic goals are set and performance measured in terms of ever-increasing corporate profits—in other words, by how fast materials can be extracted from the Earth and turned into consumer products and, ultimately, waste.

The current consumer culture is no longer geared toward the satisfaction of basic necessities, but has ventured into the nebulous realm of claiming to be able to satisfy our wildest desires. Contemporary capitalism has made the United States spiritually poverty stricken. Adam Smith[2] wouldn't recognize it—and he would have despised the runaway consumerism that is its right arm. It is refreshing to read what John Stuart Mill[3] had to say about this more than one hundred-fifty years ago; and then, wondering what level of discomfort has to be experienced before contemporary society comes to the same conclusion?

Mill was extremely uncomfortable with aspects of a prosperous, growing economy that advocated "trampling, crushing, elbowing, and treading on each other's heels."[4] He wrote that after necessities had been provided for the masses, the nations of the world should accept that condition as constant and embrace the "stationary state," where human progress would take place in realms outside of economics, in intellectual and aesthetic culture, ethical and social progress, and the arts of living.[5]

Individual happiness, well-being, and self-improvement were Mill's criteria for a good society, and he clearly indicated that these things are not necessarily measured solely by material goods. According to Mill, a stationary state might be a highly desirable society, as the pace of economic activity would moderate and allow more attention to be focused on the individual and their intrinsic development.

It's not like we need to throw the baby out with the bathwater. We do, though, need to take a long, hard look at where we are going—and why. When a culture's stories die, it dies. This is why it is critical that we write a new script. This script will have some big changes in the story line. It will be a blueprint for a New American Dream.[6] It is noteworthy that during the years surrounding the Great Depression, another time period when there was an opportunity to revision the social fabric, Arthur Olaus Dahlberg emerged as a widely read and influential theorist of Liberation Capitalism. He advocated more time spent with family, friends, the community, in nature, learning, teaching, worship, appreciation, and play. This would, he felt, invigorate working class culture and lead to a different kind of progress and a new understanding of human and national development.

One of the central thrusts of life on the farm was building a community economy. Rather than competitive one-upmanship, we practiced cooperative sharing. We believed that the exchange of goods, services, and labor in the free market didn't have to mean mindless consumerism or eternal exploitation of peoples and natural resources. We were looking for broader, more visionary systems for a radically reshaped society.

The big gestalt for me was the day that I realized that there was no "other"—that *I* was the one who had to change. If every age has its character then, as Erich Fromm suggested, my search for meaning and a more sustainable way of life was a struggle of character. I had to move out of my little, self-contained "me" and into a broader, more inclusive "we." And I had to take responsibility for my own lifestyle choices. There was no nebulous "other" out there to blame. If I got dragged along by the consumer tide, it was my own fault. To be able to take this kind of strong stand meant that I had to cultivate the qualities of Fromm's ideal, the mature, "productive character." I had to become someone "who loves and creates, and for whom being is more important than having."[7]

Was the answer to give everything up and live an ascetic life? This extreme view wasn't sufficiently integral for me. I felt that there must be some middle ground, a practical way to live within Earth's means and within society without conspicuous consumption.

Sustainable Consumption

Facing the challenges of consumption requires no less than facing the root question of life, *What is meaningful?* Another rather pragmatic way of asking this question is to consider what constitutes the opposite of waste. If the endless quest for novelty—more new stuff—only brings an endorphin crash once it is attained, there has to be a more enduring pleasure stemming from a deeper sense of satisfaction. As I began my tenure on the farm, I discovered that this was gratitude—appreciation. I began to cultivate a sense of delight in things without taking anything from them. This state of mind couldn't be practiced in fast-forward any more than stopping to smell the flowers could be scheduled. Every countryside, town, and city that had room enough for wonder offered another opportunity for gratitude.

Sustainable consumption is a new vision for consumption that meets the needs of both present and future generations for goods and services in ways that are economically, socially, and environmentally sustainable.[8] Robert G. Dunn, author of *Identifying Consumption,* suggests transforming commodities back into meaningful objects and experiences. Movements such as slow food and fair trade products, for instance, don't only help the producers. By establishing a connection with human producers, it helps the purchaser, too, by connecting him or her with meaning. Likewise, when we produce some of our own goods and services, they are naturally meaningful objects and experiences.

One of the things I learned on the farm is that any community is only as strong as its weakest members. Whereas, in the fast pace of modern life, a community's weaker members become marginalized, there was opportunity for substantial growth and integration in a small communal setting. The farm was, in Victor Turner's words, "an independent domain of creative activity."[9] When someone performed below their potential on the farm, the consequences were shared by all of us. And the consequences could be dire. A failed garden meant no food. Not getting the firewood into the woodshed meant cold living quarters. There was a direct relationship between one's ability to perform and the quality of life. Existentialism ceased to be an abstract philosophical concept. We lived it. I was the sum total of my choices. The responsibility for my life was mine.

Each of us on the farm awoke to this gestalt in their own time and way—but we all awoke to it. It was implicit in our lifestyle to awaken to our responsibilities to self and others. When one awakened, more of their human potential was necessarily tapped and, incrementally, even the weaker links in our community stepped up to the plate. There were no excuses. When I realized how intimately responsible I was for my own life, it was hard not to engage with that life—to live it more fully and more productively.

Conservation and Stacking Functions

No longer content to participate in the world solely as a representative of my earning potential and spending activity—as a consumer—I was intent on reclaiming my humanness. Making things with our hands is part of what makes us human. I made so many things on the farm with my hands. I gardened, prepared homemade meals, sewed, played several musical instruments, and cleaned stalls. One of my favorite memories, though, is of hooking rugs. Thirty years later, I still have those hooked rugs all around my Hermitage in California. They took a long time to make, but they have withstood an incredible amount of wear, and are still beautiful and serviceable. If I had bought them at retail prices, they would have been prohibitive. I paid for them, though, with some hours in a rocking chair, sitting in front of a woodstove, watching my small children play in the snow just outside the window.

When garments wore out, I tore them into long strips, which I then rolled into huge balls of color and texture. When I had enough balls, I began to crochet the rugs with a large wooden rug hook. My husband had made the hook out of maple, sanding and polishing it to a high sheen. That hook gave life to the project as the rugs began to take form. Each new concentric circle of the rugs gave them broader, more vibrant character.

Rug making embodied a number of permaculture principles, most notably *conservation* and *stacking functions*. Conservation means using only what is needed. Stacking functions means getting many uses from a single element in one's system. We needed rugs to keep the chilly floors in the old Vermont farmhouse warm. By making them out of old, worn clothing, we used no virgin resources. The function of the cloth was stacked from having been clothing to becoming rugs. And the benefits went beyond meeting my individual and family needs. They extended to society, and the Earth as a whole, in terms of lessening environmental impact from resource extraction and manufacturing.

Conservation and stacking function values were also addressed through the way that I bedded my horse stalls. Wood shavings were pricey and took eons to decompose into organic matter. Straw was also expensive and wound around the pitchfork tines, making stall cleaning tedious. I taught philosophy courses at a local college and noticed how much paper was thrown away. It occurred to me that shredded paper might make good stall bedding. I started bringing home armloads of paper from the waste bins at the college and shredded away. The horses loved their new beds. The stalls were fluffy and dry and the horses could wiggle down into little nests that they made by rolling in the shredded paper. It was easy to muck out and composted perfectly.

Shredded paper counts as brown matter in composting which is essential, especially during the growing season, when compost piles can easily err in the direction of too much green matter. Shredded paper is also an excellent carbon source for the bacteria and other decomposer-critters in the compost pile. As I found a simple pleasure in connecting with the land through changing my stall bedding habits, I participated in ecological restoration and an opportunity to heal the local environment. It was a win-win situation.

There were lots of little ways, too, that I began to address conservation and stacking functions in those years in Vermont. We had more or less ten people in residence on the farm at any given time, plus myriad numbers of children. This made a lot of dishes to wash every day. We had opted away from the use of appliances such as dishwashers and vacuum cleaners, choosing instead to handwash dishes and use nonelectrical floor cleaning tools, in order to reduce our discretionary power consumption.

One of the most annoying things about Vermont winters is frozen water pipes—and ours were certainly no exception. One morning as we geared up to do kitchen duty after breakfast, the drain pipe from the kitchen sink was frozen—again. Despite our best efforts to keep the pipe insulated, nothing we did could triumph over long weeks of subzero temperatures. This particular morning, it occurred to me that we should just remove the drain pipe and let the sink drain into a five-gallon bucket beneath the sink. I grabbed a pipe wrench and had at it! In a matter of minutes, I had torqued the pipe off and placed a big, deep bucket with a sturdy handle under the open drain. Sometimes necessity really *is* the mother of invention. I had produced the farm's first gray water system. We never replaced the drain pipe. We used biodegradable dish detergents that allowed us to use the gray water directly on our land. In the summer, we carried the buckets out to the gardens to water the vegetables. In the winter, the gray water got a second use when we mopped up the snow-tracked kitchen floor after the press of the morning meal.

At the philosophical Hermitage where I currently live in California, we use a very simple adaptation of this method. We, again, have chosen not to use a dishwasher, even though the number of guests in residence on any given day can be staggering. We use dishpans, inserted into the bays of the stainless steel sinks, for dishwashing. When the water needs changing, or we have finished the dishwashing, the pans are carefully carried out to the gardens. We have saved hundreds, if not thousands, of gallons of water this way—water that can be better used for drinking. Water is, nonarguably, becoming the "next oil." We are soon going to be past peak.

The World Bank reports that eighty countries now have water

shortages that threaten health while 40 percent of the world—more than two billion people—have no access to clean water. At least thirty-six states in the United States are expected to face water shortages within the next five years, according to government estimates, unless water conservation becomes a household effort. Some pilot studies indicate that widespread recycling of household gray water could cut residential water use as much as 16 percent. A simple way to participate in water conservation is going down the drain—literally.

Reciprocity

Whatever our capabilities, all humans are bodies that relate to space. Biking, walking, and public transit are choices we all can make about the way we move through the world. One of the choices made on the farm about moving through the world was to press my dressage mounts into service as carriage-driving horses.

At first, I was skeptical. A driving horse has to be bombproof, and some of the dressage horses were downright skittish. There was an old man, though, who lived down the road who was a wizard with driving horses. Floyd had grown up driving horses. His father had been a Vermont country doctor who made his house calls with a horse and buggy. I invited Floyd over to the farm and he taught us how to properly train a driving horse to be safe, sane, and stay sound. He had the patience of a saint as we made plenty of mistakes—learning as we went—as he guided us through each new competency.

My skepticism turned out to be ill-founded, as the dressage horses took to driving like fish to water. They loved it! There was nobody on their backs, and they weren't being asked to go around another twenty-meter circle in the indoor arena. They flagged their tails, snorted out their noses, and trotted merrily—for miles—up and down the hilly gravel roads. Once they were well-seasoned in the harness, we used them for the bulk of our transportation needs. I picked my children up from the bus stop every evening with a different horse. Whoever needed exercise got harnessed up for the job. I drove them into town for errands and even, occasionally, to the college where I taught. When I rode them again, after they had done a bit of driving, their backs were much stronger and more supple. They could round up under me with ease and spring off their haunches like cats. And the spookiness was gone. They had, after all, been exposed to all kinds of sights and sounds.

I wasn't producing any pollution from transportation or causing traffic congestion, accidents, or accelerating the need for new paved roads. From a permaculture perspective, the carriage-driving project embodied the concept of *reciprocity*—whereby one element benefits another element in the system. We benefited from transportation that was petroleum independent, and the dressage horses benefited from cross-training. Another win-win situation.

The Good and the Beautiful

I'm a sucker for beauty. Sometimes, I even think that I am a beauty junkie. I love beautifully designed things—things of quality that are built to last. I cringe at stark utilitarianism. We had come to the conclusion, on the farm, that our quest for the Good Life had to allow aesthetics and utility to hold hands. They had to be lovers. We were determined to recognize beauty as a quality that exists not only in material objects, but also in the way that we related to things. From the miniscule to the mammoth, we wedded utility and beauty.

A mantra we adopted in the farm kitchen was "people eat with their eyes first," meaning that every dish that came to the table should be as good to look at as it was to eat. Pies had lattice tops and fluted edges, entrees wore herb garnishes, and dinner plates were adorned with edible flowers. Wood was stacked carefully in interesting patterns in the sheds, classical music played softly in the barns, and we worked hard to get our hay to turn out "pretty"—meaning vibrantly green and fluffy.

The indoor riding arena on the farm was like a cathedral. I rejected any metal building designs or mass-manufactured kits. Mine was stick built by a local craftsman who made his living putting up natural wood buildings. The locals undoubtedly thought that I was crazy to put such care into a "barn," always driving by very slowly and crooning their necks to see each day's progress. It was an all-wooden structure, built from lumber that had been cut by the local sawmill. Kip, the builder, handmade the trusses and recycled enough tiny hand-blown glass windows from an old church in the area that we were able to put them—up high—around all four sides. Riding in that arena, in the late afternoon, when the golden light streamed through those delicate little panes was about as good as it gets.

The building had an implicit "cradle to cradle," or regenerative, design, through our careful use of all natural and recyclable materials. It was practical. It was beautiful. And it stood there, in the middle of the farm, as a good example of conscious consumption. Since I had begun to see myself as a caretaker of creation, my arena was an icon of investing in caring. The lumber had come from local yields and been milled just down the road; the income that Kip earned from working his craft supported his family in our local community; and the old church windows, that otherwise would have been discarded, found new use. The whole project represented a flowering of local culture and economy. Yet another win-win situation.

Appropriate Scale and Diversity

A functional "stationary state," whether at the household or community level, can only be achieved through realistic assessments of what is doable with the available time, skills, and money. This is the permaculture principle of *appropriate scale*. If this can be accomplished hand-in-hand with the permaculture principle of *diversity*, meaning that resilience is created by utilizing multiple elements within a system, so much the better.

We, for example, had initially wanted to produce all of our own electricity for the farm. More research, though, indicated that we were not sufficiently prepared to do this with the available people, skills, and money that we had. But, we did discover that we could manage to produce a *portion* of our own electricity by constructing a dynapod, or stationary pedal-powered device. The word *dynapod* comes from the Greek words for power and foot. As we pedaled, a wooden flywheel drove an electric motor, which generated an electric current that flowed into a bank of salvaged lead-acid batteries for storage. We buried a cable that connected the batteries to a set of rather conspicuous orange outlets—indicating the off-grid energy source—in our barns and outdoor workshops. Our orange outlets then powered an array of devices, such as power tools, portable lights, and radios. We had produced our own electricity on an *appropriate scale*.

Since our dynapod only produced electricity when pedaled, we got the benefit of improved fitness as a natural consequence of the workouts. It also made great exercise for the youngsters, who would otherwise be on the verge of cabin fever when we were in the middle of a long arctic snap. But our dynapod, obviously, was no mere standard-issue exercise machine. It was a homemade power plant. So, as a matter of course, it incorporated the principle of *diversity*.

Repeating Functions

Good ideas are perennial. Like wildflowers, they just keep coming back up. You have probably noticed by now that the ideas that John Stuart Mill generated in 1848 about the "stationary state" resonate with many of the contemporary principles of permaculture.

In a broadstroke, Mill argued against ideologies that champion endless economic growth as the paramount goal of every individual—spending to the limits, or beyond, of our income, not saving, investing on margin. The year 2008 gave Americans a first-person experience of what happens when that ideology fails—when the bubbles burst and the Emperor suddenly has no clothes. Many people had no backup systems—no way to subsist without radically revisioning their lifestyles.

Backup systems are one of the backbones of sustainability. Not having sufficient backup means risking expensive emergencies that often require accruing debt to address quickly. If, for example, one has no backup system for power outages and a hurricane leaves the neighborhood without electricity for a week, it's going to be costly to rent generators. And if, on top of that, one's household budget is already stretched to the max, it means that the cost of that emergency equipment rental goes on credit cards. It's a knee-jerk model based on the unrealistic assumption that "it isn't going to happen to me." Unpreparedness is unsustainable.

If someone has enough situations for which he or she is not prepared in any given year, assuming a potentially hefty debt load to get back on one's feet is a likely outcome. Anything that one has to do in a hurry isn't going to be cost-effective. My grandmother was fond of reminding us that "haste makes waste." If, on the other hand, the permaculture principle of *repeating functions* has been built into one's overall operational plan, that person is a step ahead of the game. It's hard enough to handle life's speedbumps without exploitive credit markets being part of the equation.

The most obvious *repeating function* is saving. When we collided with large expenditures on the farm—trucks, hay wagons, repairs, upgrading wood-fired furnaces, or other unexpected speed-bumps—we self-financed. We all put a predetermined dollar figure, per week, into the general operations account. Those monies went into a "green," high-yield money market fund and our weekly contributions just sat there until we needed to take out a loan. When we took money out of the fund, we treated it as a loan to ourselves and worked out amortization tables for repaying the fund. It took some discipline—but most sustainable systems do. The money *repeated function* by primarily being a nest-egg that earned a modest return, and, secondarily, provided us with interest-free loans when we needed them.

Giving Away

At the heart of a sustainable lifestyle is the permaculture principle of *giving away*. Giving to others reinforces the bonds that lie outside of monetized commerce. *Giving away* is realized any time that we pass on time, money, or goods to others and help construct the society in which we want to live. Mill wrote, "It is only in the backward countries of the world that increased production is still an important object: in those most advanced, what is economically needed is a better distribution."[10] And there is no better distribution than sharing freely!

In Mill's stationary state, as on the farm, a gentler, less materialistic ethic existed. A reorientation of values ensured that "while no one is poor, no one desires to be richer, nor has any reason to fear being thrust back by the efforts of others to push themselves forward."[11] We shared our abundance freely on the farm, giving away dozens of fresh pies, baskets of garden produce, and big wheels of homemade cheeses to anyone in need; but the time that brought me the most joy was when I gave away Toy.

Little Toy came bouncing into the world, all bling and sparkle, totally unexpected, one early summer morning. I went out to take grain buckets up to the top pasture where two old mares were turned out to graze. Both of the old broodmares had given us many good quality foals over the years—big, strong, able-bodied, sound-minded horses that were used in my dressage program, as well as for work on the farm. The two mares had gotten too old to be asked to continue having foals and were enjoying a pleasant retirement of giving the farm children bareback rides and lolling around in their summer loafing sheds. But, on this particular morning, there, suckling on my thirty-two-year-old broodmare, was a tiny, animated ball of energy. I had noticed that the mare had looked rotund and it seemed as though her bag was a bit larger, but I just attributed it to the abundant green pasture grass and spring hormones. In thinking about it, though, I remembered that the old black stallion had gotten out of his turnout one afternoon late last summer and, well, I guess he had quite a tryst!

I named the foal Precious Toy, because she was tiny and looked like a precious plaything. Her mama, Maylen, was so proud of her and telescoped her neck as if to say, "See, I can still produce beautiful babies!" So many things ran through my mind. Would the old mare have enough milk to sustain the new foal? Would she debilitate herself trying to raise her new charge? How would the other broodmare react to the new addition in their retirement quarters? Nature, though, has a way of working all of this out if we can get out of the way. The pasture where they were was knee deep in rich, lush timothy and a fresh water brook bubbled along the edge of it. For my part, I could increase her grain ration and then just leave her alone with her new baby to form a loving maternal bond.[12] I went back down to the farmhouse with the news. The children were, of course, delighted. They grabbed a pair of binoculars and ran up to a hill overlooking the top pasture and watched the mare and foal's first morning together. They drew pictures, wrote stories, and sang songs about our new addition—the Precious Toy.

By fall, Toy was ready to be handled, socialized with humans, and, eventually, weaned from Maylen. As I had worried, the lactation had been hard on Maylen, but she seemed content. She had meaning—a soul-felt purpose—in her life again. Though thin, there was a sparkle in her old eyes. The years passed and Toy morphed from a foal into a horse—except that she was really tiny. Maylen's advanced age had undoubtedly contributed to the foal being so small and not as sturdy as the foals Maylen had produced as a younger broodmare. I started Toy under saddle and she enjoyed being ridden, but she could only carry a petite rider and she didn't have sufficient strength for the rigorous demands of either dressage or farm work. What to do?

The aged mare might not have been able to give Toy size and strength, but she had stamped her with a great mind. Toy had a stellar temperament and was literally unflappable. So when the local hippotherapy program contacted me to ask if I had any quiet horses that they could use in their program several days a week, I told them about Toy. They came to the farm and worked with her several days a week for months, seeing how she would handle side-walkers, wobbly riders, being in a small arena with other horses, and so forth. She was like a fish in water. So it was decided they would use her three days a week in their program.

It was perfect—she was bombproof and perfectly comfortable with the therapeutic environment, and the work required of her was light and easy. She blossomed with the attention and enjoyed "going off to her career" three days a week, always returning to the farm relaxed and content. After about a year, I learned that one of the young clients had fallen in love with Toy and wanted to buy her.

The young woman had sufficient means, so I knew that Toy would be well provided for. Since the rider was moderately disabled, the work would be light and, most importantly, Toy would be very, very loved. I agreed to sell her. I transferred the registry papers, legalizing the change of ownership—and then I tore up the check.

A Dozen Things You Can Do

- Save pint-sized glass jars and lids and use them to carry drinking water with you to work or on trips. This eliminates having to buy corporate-interest, plastic-bottled water.
- When you consider purchasing an item, develop a habit of asking yourself whether your incentive for buying it is really based on *need*—or just *want*. Getting clear about this distinction will reduce impulse buying.
- Consider buying large equipment cooperatively with neighbors. For example, why not share a lawnmower, chainsaw or snow blower between three or four households? Think about making the same cooperative arrangements with large recreational items such as canoes or mountain bikes.
- Become a beauty junkie. Gather large, full bouquets of wildflowers and place them all around your home. You can get interesting large vases at area secondhand stores for pennies.
- Tear old clothing into strips, which you then roll into balls for crocheting circular area rugs. You can get gorgeous wooden rug hooks, individually freehand created by William Schmidt at *Turn of the Century* (Mansfield, Ohio).
- Replace your commercial kitty litter with shredded waste paper. Shred old mail and newspaper to make kitty a recycled, biodegradable litter box.
- Put a dishpan in each of the bays of your kitchen sink and use them to hand-wash dishes. Use a biodegradable dish detergent and you can use the gray water on plants in your yard and gardens.
- Lavender, daylilies, squash blossoms, violets, roses and nasturtiums are all edible flowers. Use them to add a festive garnish to dinner plates. And eat them too!
- Support your local merchants, contractors, and business professionals. Taking your dollar out of town to save a few cents isn't cost-effective in the long run. If you want to keep your local town's economy healthy and alive, you need to support it.

- Open a savings account and make regular deposits into it in order to establish a fund for self-financing future large purchases. For example, rather than taking out a bank loan to buy a car, "lend" yourself the money from the savings fund and return interest-free payments right back into the fund again.
- Pay it forward by asking that a good deed be repaid by having it done to others instead of to you. This can be really contagious and, after a while, whole neighborhoods can get involved.
- When implementing home improvement projects, try to implement cradle-to-cradle designs, by creating systems that are not just efficient but essentially waste-free.

6

The Spiritual Economy

*The propensity to truck, barter and exchange one
thing for another is common to all men, and
to be found in no other race of animals.*

—Adam Smith

Bartering, or the exchange of goods and services without money, has
seen a resurgence with the sluggish economy and struggling financial
system, becoming an increasingly common solution to tighter family budgets. In July 2009, consumers listed nearly 142,000 ads in
the barter section of Craigslist, a 96 percent increase from the year
before, according to site statistics. While approaching your car me-
chanic about exchanging a weekend of pet-sitting services for minor
repairs may be unfamiliar territory to some, most people are already
familiar with the basics of barter. "We barter in other ways all the
time," insists Jeanne Hurlburt, a professor of sociology at Louisiana
State University. "If I give you something, I expect a favor of equal
or greater value in return. Every relationship has give and take." You
might mow an elderly neighbor's lawn in exchange for some tomatoes from her garden, for example, or swap must-read books among
friends with similar tastes.

An old African proverb states, "He who wants to barter, usually knows what is best for him." Barter gets at the difference between money and wealth. Money is a symbol that expresses how we value ourselves and others, and also represents society's values at a particular time and place in history. Wealth, on the other hand, is a state of consciousness that represents generosity.

Our entire human financial structure began with barter. Our current business model started when individuals saw an opportunity to be of service by offering their excess crops to neighboring communities, in exchange for a commensurate portion of something that they needed. The exchange of goods or services was not designed to generate profit, but to benefit all parties involved. According to the World Business Academy, that is still the fundamental role of business: to be of service to society.

The fundamental problem with Wall Street and corporate America is that they have forgotten the reason that business exists. Profit is built into the market as a necessary component of the transactions, but when it is seen as the *only* reason, society inevitably loses its way. Success in life, as well as success in business, lies in conscious participation in the expression of abundance and creativity, not merely for one's own sake, but for others in society. This model of reward, primarily through service rather than money, is rooted in believing that there is enough for everyone and that no one is better than, nor lower than, anyone else.

Barter is a great equalizer. Since it is established upon need instead of greed, the value of something is relative to it being needed. This changes the playing field considerably. We have this rather stratified view of professional worth, thinking that white collar work, for example, is more valuable—and, therefore, should be paid more—than blue collar work. In a barter-based system, those lines get blurry. If, for example, you have broken water pipes and there is water spraying all over your kitchen, you need a plumber much more than you need a lawyer. You are, therefore, going to be very willing to exchange your premier goods and services to get your plumbing fixed. You're not going to think something like, "I don't want to trade my *really good* 'stuff' for this menial repair," saving it, instead, to trade for legal or medical services. You're going to be present with what's happening. And you're going to recognize the plumber's worth. You're going to see the value of the transaction. The playing field is leveled. All of our work is of worth, according to the needs of our neighbors.

A Good Trade

One of the best barter arrangements that we had on the farm was with old Leon and Irene Cady. The Cadys were long-in-the-tooth octogenarians whose family had lived, for several generations, on the property where we now lived. In fact, many of the locals still referred to the farm as "the old Cady place." The Cadys had no clue what sustainability was, but they loved what we were doing with their old place. In fact, they felt like it was being returned to its roots. Generations of Cadys had been raised there, beginning in the early 1800s. They had watched Vermont, through all of its growing pains, become the eclectic, innovative state that it is.

The Cady family remembered when native Vermonters John Deere patented the steel plow and Thomas Davenport the first electric motor. They remembered the rise to prominence of Burlington native John Dewey and Plymouth Notch born Calvin Coolidge. More importantly, they recounted days when cattle in the state outnumbered people, and the population was about 343,641 year-round residents. They told us, with excitement, about the year that women were first allowed to vote in town elections. And they remembered poignantly the year that poet Robert Frost chose Vermont to be his home.

The Cadys had planted the raspberry patch that still flourished on the farm and, every summer, they would come and ask to pick berries. They were a darling couple! Irene always wore a mid-calf length cotton dress and pulled her gray hair up into a bun under a large-brimmed straw hat. Leon sported a big-billed baseball cap, long sleeve seersucker shirt, and a little clip-on bowtie. They carried pails in which to pick, and hoisted their wicker picnic basket from their car into the shade under a big maple tree to keep their packed lunches cool and fresh. We always looked forward to their picking outings.

We traded them all the berries that they could pick for the chance to sit with them, in the old maple grove, while they had lunch and told us stories—lots of stories—about the old days on the farm.

One day, while eating sandwiches and drinking iced tea together, they told us about the great flood of 1927. They recounted how torrential rains had begun on November 3, 1927. It had already been a wet October and rivers were swollen and the ground saturated. Nine inches of rain fell in a thirty-six hour period and horrendous flooding began. Though all of New England was affected, Vermont was devastated. Leon's eyes lit up like lanterns as he described the state being flooded from Newport to Bennington. Irene chimed in that eighty-five people died and 9,000 were left homeless. Many of Vermont's roads, and over 1,200 bridges, were washed away overnight.

The great flood of 1927 changed Vermont forever, as communities turned to the state, and the state to the federal government, for assistance. As the Cadys reminisced about the change that Vermont underwent as it made its way from being an independent "hermit state" to a more interdependent part of the United States, my understanding of this place I had chosen to call home deepened. I understood my neighbors better and my appreciation for my community grew. The Cadys needed berries and I needed to establish a sense of place. It was a good trade, and one that both parties looked forward to each year.

Lessons in Prosperity Consciousness

My daughter Jec loved learning history from the Cadys—and learning to play instruments by joining impromptu jam sessions on the front porch—and learning philosophy around the dinner table as we compared the relative merits of various Eastern and Western traditions. It didn't come, therefore, as a total surprise when she announced that she wanted to be home schooled.

Vermont legislation was, in the mid-1970s, quite liberal regarding home schooling, so the option was viable. It was decided that Jec would go to the local high school in the mornings to take the core courses required for graduation and spend afternoons on the farm immersed in advanced studies. Once the logistics were worked out, I panicked, wondering how we were going to locate the expertise needed for her new program. We lived very rurally and it wasn't as if we had an intellectual smorgasbord from which to choose. This is when I learned about the spiritual economy.

I decided to just put it out there—letting people in various networks know about Jec's plan—and see what happened. Then, I tried my best to get out of the way and just let things unfold. And they did—far beyond my wildest dreams. The first person to come forward was Pulitzer Prize winner and poet laureate Maxine Kumin. She had a rogue horse that needed some work under saddle and was interested in trading the training for teaching Jec to write poetry. I got the horse going well under saddle and, under Maxine's guidance, Jec published a beautiful chapbook of poetry. Others who stepped up to the plate included an MIT professor who traded his wife's dressage lessons for teaching Jec calculus and trigonometry; a Swiss music-box maker who taught Jec German in exchange for fresh garden produce and apple cider; and a New York City–based sculptor who traded teaching Jec the basic techniques of his art for a quiet country retreat at the farm.

Jec's home school portfolio helped get her into an Ivy League college with a handsome scholarship, as well. Deepak Chopra, in *The Seven Spiritual Laws of Success,* teaches that we are pure potential. And when we discover that, we have the ability to fulfill any dream we might have. Chopra links the fulfillment of our dreams to experiencing our true nature—our souls. I learned this with Jec's home-school project. Even though I had some initial apprehension, I practiced stillness and tried to stay out of my own way. Through stillness, I was able to connect to the field of pure potentiality that orchestrated an incredible host of details for me.

Chopra also reminds us to circulate whatever we have in abundance. There is nothing that does this as effectively as barter, which offered me the opportunity to trade my abundance for that of others. The word *affluence* comes from the word *affluere* which means "to flow to," and affluence means "to flow in abundance." Energy flows. Or, it stagnates. This idea is reinforced by Eric Butterworth in *Spiritual Economics* when he writes that "the goal should not be to make money or acquire things, but to achieve the consciousness through which the substance will flow forth when and as you need it."[1] He continues, "When we are consciously centered in the universal flow, we experience inner direction and the unfoldment of creative activity. Things come too, but prosperity is not just having things. It is the consciousness that attracts things."[2]

My thoughts about Jec's proposed project had vibrated with intention. I sent out a signal asking for topflight mentors to help Jec meet her educational goals. That thought attracted matching return signals as the parade of extraordinarily qualified people materialized. Years later, when I read about the Law of Attraction in Esther and Jerry Hicks's *Ask and It Is Given,* I knew exactly what they were talking about. In the book, Esther and Jerry compare the Law of Attraction to tuning a radio. If you want to listen to something on 102.7 FM, you don't expect to hear it if your radio is set to 98.7 FM. The radio waves of one frequency can only be received by a matching tuner. Well, the Law of Attraction says that the same thing is true at the level of consciousness. If we want to receive abundance in our lives, we need to set our tuners to the frequency of abundance. For me, that meant feeling the intention as if it were already manifest.

Somehow, even in my skepticism, there was another, larger part of me that *knew* that Jec's home-school program was going to work out. I didn't know *how* it was going to work out; I just had a *feeling*—something kind of transrational—that let me remain still and centered in the field of pure potentiality. I had stumbled upon the secret of the spiritual economy. I learned that, if I kept an internal locus of control, I could *choose* how I looked at the world and interpreted events. I became incrementally more independent of the ups and downs of the external world, such as my well-intentioned neighbors' worries that Jec would never get into college or my parents' concerns about her peer socialization.

I was on my way toward developing a consciousness through which things could flow as, and when, needed. Little by little, I gained the confidence to trust the spiritual economy, rather than feeling dependent upon the precarious consumer economy. Through conscious, willed participation in the expression of abundance and creativity, not merely for my own sake, but for that of others, culturally conditioned scarcity consciousness fell away. I learned that, through adopting community instead of consumerist models, there really *is* enough for everyone.

Bubbles of Debt

Knowing that there is enough for everyone is a grounded, practical approach to overcoming scarcity consciousness. It is not, however, to be confused with an abandoned, reckless "shop till you drop" attitude. If there's enough for everyone, we can just buy, buy, buy, right? Wrong! That is the carrot held out by consumer culture that gets confused for abundance. Instead, it is an egocentric position that only considers one's own self. This is directly opposed to knowing that there is enough for *everyone*. And, sadly, sometimes there isn't *really* even enough for ourselves—because we have attained our "stuff" by accruing a mountain of debt.

Debt accrual is the antithesis of participating in a spiritual economy. Credit consumers don't even ask themselves whether or not they can really afford the whole cost of, for example, a vacation or landscaping, but ask, instead, whether or not they can afford the resulting increase in their monthly bills. Their answer is invariably "yes." They are a creation of the no-money-down and low-interest incentives that proliferated in the FIRE (finance, insurance, real estate) economy of recent years.

In his 1939 book, *Business Cycles*, Joseph Schumpeter predicted trouble whenever a load of debt was "lightheartedly incurred by people who foresaw nothing but boons."[3] He was right. Now that the credit and housing bubbles have burst, unbridled debt-financed consumer spending and monthly payment models are being critically questioned.

Mainstream consumer culture wants to reinflate the credit bubble and engineer a return to "the old days." But this isn't sustainable.

When a nation's businesses and households take on too much debt and the economy stumbles, the cashflow needed for financing dries up, defaults rise, and a vicious cycle of falling incomes, asset prices, and collateral values begins. Boom-to-bust cycles end only when asset prices, debt levels, and incomes get back into balance.

When we needed a loan on the farm, we self-financed from our own coffers and then meticulously paid ourselves back so that the funds were replenished for future needs. I didn't use any credit cards. I used cold, hard cash to pay for everything. Using only cash kept the pace of my life slower. I could walk into a store and differentiate between the things that I really needed and things I just wanted. And I didn't have to worry about lots of small expenditures sneaking up on me at the end of a month since it made me think more carefully about how I spent my money. Cash was actually convenient. I don't care what the commercials for Visa say, having someone—or multiple people—in front of you in line pull out their plastic to pay for a $3.25 latte can be slow and aggravating. Everyone accepts cash as payment. And the best part was that I never spent money on interest or fees and penalties. Since I wasn't shackled by debt, I was able to follow my dreams and pursue a more creative, individualized life. A Good Life.

I went to my fortieth high school reunion just as the economy was tanking. I spent the evening talking with an old friend who had taken the "road more traveled by." She had invested heavily in all of the bubble markets; and having forsaken marriage and children, had chosen instead to claw her way up the corporate ladder to a lucrative job that she hated. Even though she earned a six-figure income, she had substantial debt. Now her retirement monies were seriously devalued, and her real estate holdings were sitting empty as qualified tenants were becoming harder and harder to find. She was approaching retirement age with the prospect of having to keep working in order to finish paying off her supersized home—which was now valued at less than her mortgage. The bank owned her cars and she had hefty credit card balances. On top of it all, her company was reorganizing in an effort to deal with recent economic declines and there was talk about cutting her position to consolidate administrative costs. Stress was eating away at her. She had traded freedom for mainstream culture's definition of "security"—and it had turned out to be another bubble that had subsequently burst.

It's part of our nature to question ourselves and I had done my fair share of that. There had been times, of course, when I had wondered if my choice to take the "road less traveled by" had been the right decision. But, in talking with my old friend, I felt my freedom. I had no debt—none. By following the principles of the spiritual, instead of consumer, economy, I had been able to live my life without accumulating debt. My home and cars were paid for. There were no student loans left lurking in the wings. I had no credit card balances. Instead of racking up debt, I had relied heavily upon barter, exchanging goods and services with others—and built some solid social capital as a natural extension of the process.

While others had diversified their portfolios, I had diversified my career interests and had worked part-time in both philosophy and dressage, thereby expressing my dual passions and keeping myself intellectually and professionally vital. No burnout. And if one source of revenue dried up, the other was always there.

My retirement plans hadn't been built around Wall Street but were, instead, rooted in the social capital I had invested in the concentric circles of my own community. No Madoff ponzi schemes. No evaporated 401(k). Most importantly, I was content and wasn't being ravaged by the gnawing effects of stress. In the words of Robert Frost, I took the road "less traveled by and that has made all the difference."[4]

The average American household's credit card debt in 1990, according to the American Bankers' Association, was $2,966. By 2007 it had risen to $9,840, and jumped to $10,700 in 2009. About 43 percent of American families spend more than they earn each year. According to a recent *USA Today* article about debt, 78 percent of baby boomers have mortgage debt, 59 percent have credit card debt, and 56 percent have car payments. From 1996 to 2007, the total number of bank credit cards increased 46 percent and credit card companies made $43 billion in income from late payment, over-limit, and balance transfer fees. Charge-off rates in January 2009 were 40 percent higher than the previous year.

Personal debt is one of those things that people like to forget about. As long as they can keep making the monthly payment, they think they'll be okay. And yet their future earnings are being eaten away at an accelerated rate, with no end in sight. Americans have never been so indebted, owing on credit cards, personal loans, student loans, and home mortgages.

Once people are sufficiently debt saturated, they begin to throw caution to the wind and just buy even more "stuff." They figure that getting their personal debt paid off is hopeless, and just begin to accept it as a normal part of their economic lives. So they keep buying—and buying. The buying actually becomes cathartic, an outlet for hidden anxieties that lurk behind all of the "new stuff." And debt-financed shopping sprees are given the thumbs up by big corporate messages telling buyers that they are stimulating an otherwise flagging economy. Consumerism has become a new type of nationalism.

Consumer Nationalism

Consumers are bombarded with public relations sound bites reminding them that they are responsible for supporting a prosperous and endlessly growing economy. We are reminded of Mill's discomfort with certain aspects of this type of thinking as he felt that it could lead to "trampling, crushing, elbowing, and treading on each other's heels."[5] Those are strong words.

We saw, however, a tragic, literal example of Mill's worst fears in November 2008 when an employee was stampeded to death on Black Friday—the biggest retail day of the year in America—as consumers stormed a Long Island Walmart in a shopping frenzy. Roughly 2,000 people gathered outside the Walmart's doors in predawn darkness, chanting "push the doors in," as the crowd pressed against the glass and the clock ticked down to the 5:00 A.M. opening.

A stampede plunged the outlet into chaos. Drunk with the excitement of bargain hunting, with credit cards in hand, shoppers trampled, crushed, elbowed, and tread on each other's heels—literally—with sufficient abandon to cost a thirty-four-year-old, innocent temporary employee his life. When shoppers were advised by store administrators that they had to leave—that an employee had been killed—they retorted by yelling, "I've been in line since Friday morning!" and they just kept shopping!

Items on sale at the store included a $798 Samsung 50-inch Plasma HDTV, a Bissel Compact Upright Vacuum for $28, and Men's Wrangler Tough Jeans for $8. This certainly wasn't a scenario that suggested a consciousness that recognized that there was enough for everybody. No spiritual economy. This was consumer economy at its worst. No sense of fair or equal exchange. Unsustainable. Would anybody *consciously* exchange a $20 discount on a TV for a man's life?

A Dozen Things You Can Do

- Expose your children to the elderly. Encourage elder men and women to share stories from their less consumer-driven generations with your children. Process these stories with your children in a way that helps them develop perspective about personal economy.

- Engage in positive visualizations regarding issues of lifestyle, prosperity, and community. Hold an intention to attract the Good Life for yourself and your loved ones.

- Create a social experiment whereby you use *only* cash for all direct purchases for a month. Notice how this experiment changes your perceptions about the value of things. Notice how this experiment helps you make a more clear distinction between those things that you *need* versus those that you *want*.

- Develop a savings habit. Put a certain amount of money into a savings account weekly. Treat this deposit just like a bill.

- Cut up your credit card. Make a budget whereby you can live within your means. If you need to purchase something online that requires "plastic" (such as airline tickets), use your bank card. (Remember that you can always self-finance an expensive airline ticket, for example, by lending yourself money from your savings account. Then, pay it back just like any other loan.)

- Make achieving freedom from debt a priority. Pay extra on the principal of your home mortgage, car loans, and any outstanding student loans. Treat these extra principal payments like a bill. This practice will not only move you toward debt freedom but also save you thousands of dollars in interest.

- Do not get lured into the trap of using a home equity loan for personal finance. This is a risky undertaking and is an unsustainable practice.

- Consider changing how you contribute toward your retirement. Instead of just routinely contributing to investment products, think about putting money toward solar panels, greenhouses, energy efficient appliances, garden equipment, and hybrid vehicles.

- Remember that it is *not* your responsibility to stimulate a recessed economy. That is hype. It is your responsibility to create a sustainable lifestyle—which, most likely, will involve *less* consumerism.
- Get active in local transition initiatives and explore the feasibility of your town establishing a local currency. These currencies are referred to as community currencies and allow an area to have a lower interest rate than the national currency.
- Use your community library. This practice eliminates the need to purchase books, thus saving paper. It also supports community library initiatives—which come under fire when municipalities have budget woes—as essential to maintaining an educated and literate population.
- Request to be taken off of all telemarketing and sales catalog lists. This saves enormous amounts of paper, as well as reduces the risk of impulse buying.

7

Getting Out of the Fast Lane

*What can be added to the happiness of a man who is
in health, out of debt, and has a clear conscience?*

—Adam Smith

I learned, while living on the farm, that investing in my own health
yielded higher returns than any other investment option. I also learned
that stress was to physical health as debt was to economic health—it
ate away at the returns of my investment. I arrived at the farm as
pretty much of a type A personality. I was impatient, time-conscious,
and ambitious. I had just stepped off the graduate school treadmill
where high achievement and meeting deadlines drove the process.
Even if it hadn't been indigenous to my nature, the rigors of the ivory
tower had morphed me into a stress junkie.

We are adaptive and, over time, we change to fit into our surroundings. The farm was a type B community. It offered a relaxed lifestyle
where people were patient and easy going. Mother Nature whittled
away any artificial sense of urgency that our human minds tried to
impose on life. Proactivity replaced reactivity under Her guidance.
More than once, I barely finished shoveling footpaths between the
barns after a huge snowstorm when it would begin to snow—hard—

again. Likewise, there were mornings in mid-June when I awoke to find our carefully planted garden seedlings killed by a late frost. There were calves born dead, injured horses and deer trampling through the berry patches. Nature was the schoolmaster. She taught me to find "the serenity to accept the things I could not change." Little by little, I noticed that my personal stress level was reducing. And, concurrently, my health was improving.

Pedal to the Metal

Stress is a normal psychological and physiological reaction to the demands of life. Our brains come hardwired with an alarm system for our protection. When our brain perceives a threat, our body releases a burst of hormones to fuel the fight-or-flight response. When the threat is gone, our bodies return to normal. Unfortunately, the nonstop stress of modern life means that our alarm systems rarely shut off. This is a big problem!

Many people caught up in the fast pace of consumer culture feel like there are too many pressures and demands on them. They lose sleep worrying about tests, schoolwork, job layoffs or debt loads. Their schedules are so tight that if they didn't eat on the run they wouldn't eat at all. Our bodies respond to stressors by activating the nervous system and specific hormones. These hormones speed up heart and breathing rates, blood pressure, and metabolism. These physical changes prepare a person to react quickly and effectively to handle emergencies.

In the correct context, the body's stress response enhances our ability to perform well under pressure. The stress response is critical, for example, when a driver has to slam on the brakes to avoid an accident. It can also be activated in a milder form when the pressure's on but there's no actual danger—like stepping up to take the foul shot that could win the game. A little of this stress can help keep us on our toes, ready to rise to a challenge. But the stress response can also cause problems when it fails to turn off and reset itself properly.

In the pace of contemporary life, stress doesn't just happen in response to things that are immediate or that are over quickly. Ongoing events, like coping with a huge mortgage or layoffs at work, cause stress, too. These long-term stressful situations produce lasting, low-level stress that runs us down. When the nervous system remains on alert to pump out extra stress hormones over long periods of time, the body's reserves are depleted, leaving a person feeling exhausted or overwhelmed, and weakening the immune system.

The old saying that stress contributes to premature aging was recently verified in a study of women who had spent many years caring for severely ill and disabled children. Long-term exposure to the stress involved in caring for the children caused these women to be physically a decade older than their chronological age.

In other research conducted by a team of forty-four scientists in ten countries, commissioned by the World Health Organization's International Agency on Cancer Research, overnight shift work has been listed as a probable carcinogen. Experts estimate that nearly 20 percent of the working population in developed countries work night shifts.

Among the first to spot the night shift–cancer connection was Dr. Richard Stevens, a cancer epidemiologist and professor at the University of Connecticut Health Center. He began in 1987 by trying to figure out why breast cancer incidence suddenly shot up starting in the 1930s in industrialized societies, where nighttime work was considered a hallmark of progress. In more recent years, several corroborating studies have found that women working at night over many years were indeed more prone to breast cancer.

Dr. Najib T. Ayas of the University of British Columbia notes that contemporary consumer culture is shifting to a twenty-four-hour-a-day, seven-day-a-week society. As a result, people are not sleeping like their grandparents did. As the press of consumer culture encroaches, a good night's sleep often loses out to answering emails, finishing up late-night projects brought home from work, and catching up on deferred household duties. Research is beginning to show that sleep deprivation is eroding health.

A large, new study, for example, provides the latest in a flurry of evidence suggesting that the nation's obesity epidemic is being driven, at least in part, by a corresponding decrease in the average number of hours that Americans are sleeping, possibly by disrupting hormones that regulate appetite. The analysis of a nationally representative sample of nearly 10,000 adults found that those between the ages of thirty-two and forty-nine who sleep less than seven hours a night are significantly more likely to be obese.

Physiologic studies also suggest that a sleep deficit may put the body into a state of high alert, increasing the production of stress hormones and driving up blood pressure, a major risk factor for heart attacks and strokes. Moreover, people who are sleep-deprived have elevated levels of substances in the blood that indicate a heightened state of inflammation in the body, which has also recently emerged as a major risk factor for heart disease, stroke, cancer, and diabetes.

Downshifting

Life on the farm moved slowly and methodically. Although our days were long and we worked hard, nobody rushed. We got up before sunrise and, after stoking the woodstoves and steeping several pots of tea, we spent an hour in gymnastics. I did yoga. Others chose tai chi or dance. Afterwards, we had quiet time for a half-hour, during which people could meditate, pray, read, or contemplate. We sat quietly together, just as the sun peeked over the hilltops, with candles and incense as our silent companions. I chose meditation and began what became a lifetime practice of "observing my mind." I noticed in the early years on the farm that it was hard for me to sit still so early in the morning. My still unreformed type A persona wanted to jump out of bed and hit the ground running. It was only after years of meditation practice that the light bulb went off for me and I noticed that my days were actually going much more smoothly than they had when I had just gotten up and jumped into the day at turbo speed.

I began to be active from within a context of stillness. Mindfulness grew. The morning yoga and meditation moved me from my habitu-ated beta brain state, ranging between 13–40 cycles per second, into an alpha brain state, cycling between 7–12 cycles per second. Huge difference. While beta waves were perfect for acing exams, playing sports, and defending my dissertation, slower alpha waves were the antidote for stress. Where beta represented arousal, alpha represented nonarousal. Lower brain waves equaled lower stress levels.

As my stress level reduced, I noticed that I had more energy. It was clear, creative energy that refreshed me, instead of chaotic, incoherent activity that exhausted me. According to traditional Chinese medicine, this type of vital energy is called *chi*. There are two broad categories of chi: prenatal and postnatal.

Prenatal chi is transmitted directly to us at the time of conception. It is a gift from our parents. The quality of prenatal chi determines our general constitution—whether we are strong and healthy or weak and sickly. As we progress through life, we draw upon this prenatal chi, first to develop and grow, and then just to survive. Since there is, however, a finite amount, we gradually exhaust the supply and our bodies begin to deteriorate.

I came into the world with prenatal chi to spare. I was incredibly resilient and had an iron constitution. I could work like a Trojan, take a short nap, and get up and do it all again. Until—one day I hit a wall. I noticed that bales of hay got heavier, days seemed longer. But after discovering that I could consciously shift brain states, I tapped into a whole new source of energy—the ability to generate postnatal chi.

Postnatal chi is a renewable resource. Peter Ragnar says, "Basically, we come into this life with a battery that has a certain amount of juice in it. I call this *prenatal* chi. If you don't do a thing and you just continue to run with your lights on and the radio blaring, eventually the battery will wear out, depending upon how much demand you put on it. . . . However, if you plug the battery in at night and you charge it, there's no end in sight—that's *postnatal* chi."[1] Consumer culture, lived in the fast lane, doesn't provide ample opportunities for generating postnatal chi. Consequently, people exhaust the reserves of their prenatal chi, and begin to fall apart.

Swallowing the Sun

Falling apart in America is currently so commonplace that it's considered normal. According to the Center for Disease Control and

Prevention, 16 percent of adult Americans have high cholesterol; 10 percent have diabetes; 11 percent suffer from heart disease; and 66 percent are overweight or obese. A recent Reuters report announced that the use of antidepressant drugs in the United States doubled between 1996 and 2005 and the National Institute of Mental Health reports that over 18 percent of the adult population in the United States suffer from anxiety disorders in any given year.

Recent numbers released by Medco Health Solutions, Inc., indicate that more than half of all insured Americans are taking prescription medicines regularly for chronic health problems. And that's only the *insured* Americans. The number would be even higher if it included the 46.6 million, or 15.9 percent, of Americans who lack health coverage. Americans are so conditioned to believe that life is just a slow march from the womb and the tomb that they don't even question it when they begin to fall apart. Philosophers, though, are of a different ilk. We question everything. Plus, I couldn't reconcile falling apart with my vision for a Good Life.

As I learned to relax my mind and began reducing my stress levels, I discovered that I was generating—instead of depleting—postnatal chi. I was recharging my battery. My vitality soared. The life force could be seen in my eyes and heard in my voice. My body moved without hesitation and my posture became regal.

If we are conscious enough, we can change what happens with our bodies. We can preserve our body or we can kill it. I had, previously, been killing myself with my thoughts—with stress. I was a product of my own unconscious cause-and-effect cycles. As I became incrementally more conscious of my thoughts and developed more cognitive fluidity, a dynamic and powerful energy built up inside of me. I was different. I radiated as if I had swallowed the sun. As I added more conscious energy and life force to my physical organism, I noticed old thoughts about "limitation" dropping away. More freedom.

I downloaded even more postnatal chi from food and air. I discovered that it was not just *what* I ate, but *how, when,* and *with whom.* The farm was a Slow Food haven, nestled into a nation starved for time, bloated with fast food, and mostly ignorant of where, how, and by whom their food was produced or prepared. Our feasts of the fields centered around enjoying our farm-grown produce in the company of one another. American macaroni-and-cheese culture paled in comparison to a stroll through one of our verdant gardens, gathering fragrant pea blossoms and lemon verbena. Even the gooiest, most seductive prepackaged, processed deserts were no match for our sweet treats.

My favorite was ice cream—vanilla with fresh-picked orchard fruits stirred into it. It was easy enough to make. It just took a little time and some advance planning. I'd start with a gallon of cooled milk from one of our Jersey cows. Jerseys are a small dairy breed best known for the high butterfat content of their milk—perfect for making ice cream. If the milk had cooled enough, the cream would have risen to the top. I'd mix an equal amount of cream and milk together and, in a large pan, bring it just to the boiling point and stir in some maple sugar. Sometimes I'd use eggs and sometimes I wouldn't, depending on whether we wanted an ice cream that was French custard style or one that was Philadelphia style. Either way, then the mixture got spooned into the hand-cranked ice cream maker.

There was never any lack of youngsters under foot begging to turn the crank. They would all take fifteen minutes shifts, spelling each other to try to hurry the ice cream along. When it was ready, I'd scrape it from the churn and add strawberries, peaches, cherries, or whatever other fruit was in season. It always got eaten, soft and runny, before it ever made it into the freezer to set up. We'd savor every spoonful.

When nutrients from high-quality slow foods combined with fresh, clean air, precious postnatal chi was produced. My daughter and I went for long, slow walks through the wooded hills, pausing to sit beside tumbling streams and baby waterfalls. We said that we were out "looking for chi" and would sniff our way along until the air had a certain quality that we associated with chi. We found these spots in humid natural settings. When we found them, we would sit down and practice pranayama, or breath control, until a sense of well-being washed over us.

And we loved the way that the air, just after a summer thunder-storm, made us feel, too. Our "chi spots" were places rich in nega-tive ions, important odorless, tasteless, and invisible molecules that produced biochemical reactions once they reached our bloodstreams. The negative ions increased our serotonin, relieving stress and boost-ing our daytime energy. We literally filled our nostrils with new life force. No pills, no prescriptions, no products. Just fresh air—and postnatal chi.

Blue Zones

The farm was a micro–Blue Zone. Blue Zones are places in the world where higher percentages of people enjoy remarkably long, healthy, full lives. According to National Geographic Explorer Dan Buettner, in his recently authored *The Blue Zones,* common denominators of the world's healthiest, longest-lived people include putting their loved ones first, spirituality, and having found meaning in their lives. Buettner organized the behaviors of Blue Zone residents into four main categories, one of which was belonging to the right tribe.

There is a trend in consumer culture toward social isolation. If you drive down any American street at 9:00 P.M., you can see the iridescent glow of the TV or computer screen in people's windows. Fifteen years ago, the average American had three good friends. Now it's down to two. Research indicates that isolation shaves good years off of our lives. We are social animals.

According to Buettner, all of the world's longest-lived people were born into, or consciously chose to associate with, the right people—their tribe. If we eat with people who eat healthy food, we're more likely to eat healthy food; if the friends we spend the most time with exercise, we probably will, too. But the reverse is true, also. The Framingham Studies indicate that if our three best friends are obese, there's a 50 percent better chance that we'll be obese.

Living on a communal farm put me in touch with my tribe from the get-go. From morning to night, I was in the midst of like-minded peers. It wasn't always easy. We were a tribe keen upon exploring the territory between our conditioning and our consciousness. We had all come to the farm with very different backgrounds and life schemas, yet we had come with a shared interest in self-growth and actualization.

Ritual is part of what holds tribes together. We learned early on that we would have to establish our own rituals—apart from our individually conditioned expectations—if we were going to be true to our intentions. One of my favorite of these rituals was the rite of passage celebrated with our young girls when they became a woman.

Having lived so close to the earth, these girls were no strangers to the Goddess. Mother Earth abided in their hearts: they instinctually recognized her as the creatrix who manifested the dancing forms of consciousness. Since they had been raised to believe that women were fully equal, they had no misgivings about becoming a woman. They didn't harbor hidden concerns that their initiation was a sentence into second-class citizenry. Unlike my generation, who had a tough row to hoe ahead of them—struggling to negotiate a hall of mirrors created by patriarchal social values—these women saw themselves incarnating into their Goddess nature, the Divine Mother. She had come from nowhere, meaning that there was never a time She did not exist: she was eternal, immanent, and accessible.

Since our tribe had consciously chosen to live without imposing any sense of sexual shame, the young girls were comfortable when they began menstruating. As soon as one would announce this event, we planned her rite of passage. We all worked together and crafted a crown, made from stiff-painted cardboard onto which we pasted buttons, colorful images, glitter, and lace. Depending on the season, we made a garland from either fresh flowers, acorns and dried flowers, or tiny gilded pinecones for the initiate to wear around her neck. The older women on the farm worked feverishly to hand sew a simple, flowing dress—beautiful in its simplicity. The men took pains to construct a makeshift throne from an old chair, adorning it for new royalty. And, of course, the kitchen bustled with preparations for the upcoming celebration. Sugar and spice and everything nice went into cakes, cookies, pies, and tarts.

Songs and poems were written and practiced, stories were prepared to be told, and skits were rehearsed in order to be play-worthy by the appointed day. When that day came, it was like a mini-Beltane celebration. Our Queen was crowned and she sat upon her throne as we entertained her—a royal court. We sang and danced; shared stories and poetry; enjoyed new music; and watched extemporaneous one-act plays. Treats were served on carefully garnished platters and teas in little demitasse cups.

From start to finish, preparation to party, social isolation was overridden by social integration. Like other Blue Zones around the world, we had established social norms that brought us together in intergenerational, supportive ways. We were good friends, spiritual family, celebrating our shared lives.

When a House Is Not a Home

Malcolm Gladwell, author of *The Tipping Point,* would call it the *power of context*: that human beings are a lot more sensitive to their environment than they may seem. The power of context indicates that many things I believe, in large part, are due to where and when—and with whom—I was. In other words, many of the things that I believe are due to the tribe in which I chose to belong.

The farmhouse was massive. It was one of the oldest houses in Brookfield, Vermont, built in 1786, when New England families were large. Thus, the eight bedrooms. Had we not used it communally, it would have been way "too much house" for a single family. The repairs and renovations on the old place would have cost a fortune, keeping a single-family household working overtime at the office just to make enough money to get the work done. They would have spent so much time at the office that they wouldn't even have been able to spend much time in the house they were working to refurbish.

This is true of many homeowners in contemporary culture. They are "over-housed" to the point that the actual number of hours that they spend in their home per week is significantly reduced by the number of hours that they have to spend away from their home—on the job—in order to pay for it! At this point, a house is no longer a home. It's a place to store "stuff."

Cohousing options are becoming more popular, in response to recent economic downturns, since people are being drawn to their efficiency and implicit support systems. Cohousing communities can be as simple as old-fashioned neighborhoods created with more ingenuity and intentionality. They bring together the value of private homes with the benefits of more sustainable living through shared common facilities and equipment—kitchens, laundry rooms, recreational areas, gardens, workshops, lawnmowers, snow blowers, chain saws—and good connections with neighbors.

The modern theory of cohousing originated in Denmark in the 1960s when Bodil Graae published "Children Should Have One Hundred Parents." His ideas spurred a group of fifty families to develop the cohousing project Sættedammen, which is the oldest known cohousing community in the world. Another shaker and mover who generated interest in cohousing was Jan Gudmand Høyer, a Harvard architectural student who published "The Missing Link between Utopia and the Dated One-Family House" in 1968.

The size of one's home is a big contributor to stress levels. When one's whole life is consumed with excessive—and expensive—maintenance, repair, and upkeep, stress mounts up. Ciji Ware's book, *Rightsizing Your Life,* fans the flames of the growing rightsizing movement. According to Ware, rightsizing is achieving a harmony between your physical environment and your desired lifestyle. It's not downsizing. Rather, Ware defines rightsizing as "a conscious, practical and psychological evolution in the way one lives one's life—a process that enables people to create new surroundings."[2] It involves a conscious choice to change our relationship with our home.

The McMansion—the Hummer-house—is losing its allure. It's time to rethink home ownership. Do we actually buy *homes*, places to *live*. . . . or *houses, commodities* that are held for their investment value? February 2009 foreclosure filings were up almost 30 percent from February 2008. This translates into one in every 440 U.S. homes having received a foreclosure filing in February.

Real estate values around the nation have collapsed, and sales of foreclosed and "underwater" homes accounted for nearly 20 percent of the nation's 2009 home sales. Another 11 percent were short sales, in which homeowners owed more in mortgage debt than their homes were worth. About $3.3 trillion in home equity was erased in 2008, according to Humphries. More than $6 trillion in value has been lost since the housing bubble peaked in 2005.

The average American single family home swelled from 983 square feet in 1950 to 2,349 square feet in 2004—a 140 percent increase in size. That's a pretty hefty increase in maintenance, repair, upkeep, taxes, insurance, and mortgage costs. In order to make enough money to meet the financial obligations incurred, the owner has to work time and overtime—hours each week that they are not even in the home. Basic housekeeping duties either get relegated to service providers— lawn and yard care, cleaning, laundry—or done late at night by already exhausted owners. Repairs and maintenance get contracted out to local handymen. Taking care of the place is either expensive or exhausting—or both. At this point, a house is not a home. It's a headache, literally.

Creating, instead, a micro-Blue Zone—a new type of surroundings—is a viable option for the *New* American Dream. Consciously creating a life that factors in stress reduction invests in our health and serenity. In the big picture, that's a higher return than any of the recent market bubbles have yielded.

A Dozen Things You Can Do

- Start a seed sprouting kitchen garden. Sprouting at home assures freshness and saves a lot of money. It provides sprouts without any plastic packaging or long distance transportation.
- Learn how to make dandelion blossom jelly. There are plenty of good recipes for this on the Internet, but I'll bet your grandmother has some good ones, too! This jelly is really good, with a taste and texture very similar to honey.
- Join the Slow Food Movement. Stop eating on the run and re-order your day so you have time to actually sit down and eat your meals slowly and quietly. Make this a time priority.
- Get eight hours sleep every night. Again, make this a time priority. Readjust your schedule to make this happen.
- Find a window of quiet time for yourself in the mornings before the press of the day begins. Don't schedule early morning appointments. Make a slower entry into each day.
- Recharge your battery regularly. Learn and practice ways to generate postnatal chi.
- Learn and practice some basic pranayama techniques.
- Spend time in mountains, waterfalls, and beaches in order to gain access to negative ions. Negative ions, in the bloodstream, produce biochemical reactions that help to alleviate depression, relieve stress, and boost daytime energy.
- Rightsize your living space. If you determine that your home is too large, consider cohousing options whereby you share some of your space with others. This could involve renting out some rooms, creating communal living arrangements, offering guest lodging to out-of-towners, or trading room and board for work.
- Find your tribe! Make a real effort to meet, and associate with, people who embody the qualities you want to enhance in yourself. Chose your friends consciously. Don't just hang out with whoever is handy. Make a concerted effort to spend time with people who contribute to your own evolution.

- Create rituals that will add meaning to your life. Observe these rituals faithfully. Teach the importance of ritual to your children.
- Critically assess your living space. Is your house a place to *live* or a place to store "stuff"? Be radically honest in this assessment. What can you do to assure that your house is really a *home* and not an investment commodity?

8

Playing More and Paying Less

Leave all the afternoon for exercise and recreation, which are as necessary as reading. I will rather say more necessary because health is worth more than learning.

—Thomas Jefferson

We think of recreation as play. And it is. It refreshes our minds and bodies after periods of work. Etymologically, the word goes back to the Latin *recreatio* that means "to re-create." When we recreate, we literally re-create ourselves. We become new bodies and new minds. We open up space for new ideas to pour in and new perspectives on how we see things become available.

Recreation signals the body to regenerate from the cellular level on up. The brain functions as a computer and when the body operates optimally, there is constant feedback from the brain to all of the organs and other body parts, facilitating continual regeneration. The body, though, can't operate optimally without regular recreation. It's a critical part of the mix for living the Good Life. Recreation re-creates our brains: neurons crave novelty.

Americans, though, aren't all that good at recreating. A 2003 survey by Management Recruiters International of 730 U.S. executives found that 47 percent surveyed wouldn't use all of their vacation time, and 58 percent said that the reason was perceived job pressures. This same study also found that 35 percent said that they had too much work to take a vacation and that 17 percent felt that their boss was not supportive of employees taking all of their vacation days.

In another study by *Expedia.com* in 2003, it was estimated that there was $21 billion in unused vacation time for that year. After repeating the study in 2004, they found that 35 percent of employees didn't take all their time off because of job pressures. Many others are afraid to use their paid leave for fear they could be laid off or demoted if they do. It is estimated that the amount of annual vacation time actually taken has shrunk from an average of more than seven days twenty-five years ago to only four days now.

According to a survey by Harris Interactive, 30 percent of employed adults gave up vacation time they had earned, resulting in a total of 460 million unused vacation days in 2008.

Recreation Deficit

Then there is the other side of the problem. Nearly one-fourth of American workers have no paid vacation or holidays, according to a recent study from the Washington, D.C.–based Center for Economic and Policy Research, and nearly half of all private sector workers have no paid sick days.

The United States is one of the only modern countries without vacation-time minimums mandated by law. The moment, in fact, that Congressman Alan Grayson introduced the Paid Vacation Act of 2009, a roar of protest welled up within the corporate sector. No wonder the average American vacation is now down to a long weekend. Americans now work more every year than workers in most other industrialized countries. With women working longer hours each year, the average annual work time for couples is growing steadily, while recreational time—so crucial for bonding and intimacy—is diminishing.

Full time workers in most of Europe typically take seven to eight weeks of vacation and holidays each year. The European Union requires its members to set a minimum standard of four weeks paid vacation, which applies to part-time workers as well. Finland and France require six weeks paid vacation, plus additional paid holidays. Some governments even require employers to pay bonuses so that workers can afford to do more than just sit at home during their vacation time.

The London-based HSBC Group, for example, starts its England-based employees out with twenty-six vacation days plus eight public holidays each year. A U.S. employee in an American subsidiary would have to be on the job for ten years at HSBC before getting that kind of time off.

According to Harvard economist Alberto Alesina, Europeans are happier, and have less stress and insecurity, which is good for health and longevity. Supporting studies in the United States, for example, indicate that taking vacations cuts the risk of heart attacks, in male populations, in half. Also, longer, mandated vacations haven't undercut the competitiveness of other wealthy countries, and there's even evidence to suggest that they have increased their productivity.

In American "get it done yesterday" society, people's identities are tied up with their work. When asked "What do you do?" most Americans assume that the question is about what they do for work. However, in other parts of the world, that same question could have quite different meanings. It might, for example, mean "What do you do for fun?," something that might never enter an American's mind.

Most Americans no longer work to live. They live to work. America is the product of the Protestant work ethic. According the Max Weber's *The Protestant Ethic and the Spirit of Capitalism,* our contemporary attitudes toward work originated with Calvinism that taught that all men must work, even the rich, because to work was the will of God. Weber especially emphasized the popular writings of Benjamin Franklin as an example of how, by the eighteenth century, diligence in work, scrupulous use of time, and deferment of pleasure had become a part of the popular American philosophy of work.

The Puritan ethic is undeniably still alive in America today. Working hard means that you can afford to accumulate more material wealth. Working hard means that you are a "good person"—you have a "good work ethic." Having a good work ethic automatically gives people credibility in America. Americans are defined by the fruits of their labor—their car, their home, their clothing—all of these things define them: this is what one is "worth." And, this is exactly the type of "worthiness" that the Puritan work ethic was all about.

The long story short is that Americans are suffering from recreation deficit. And, when they do recreate, it may actually result in the accumulation of more debt load and, consequently, *more* stress. This is because recreation has become a commodity—and an expensive one at that. Americans *buy* recreation now, instead of *doing* it.

Disneyland is referred to, in the media hype, as "The Happiest Place on Earth"—and it might be. But the cost of that dreamed-of family trip to Disneyland is more like a nightmare. A ten-day European trip, with the family in tow, is in the same ballpark. And, even if you stay closer to home, it can be spendy. AAA's 2008 survey showed that the average American couple traveling in North America would spend about $250 per day for lodging and meals. Typically, people travel for two to five days, so this would put a modest trip for two at about $500 to $1250—and, of course, the costs go up if there are more people involved or if you are traveling with kids.

One of the greatest examples of an American oxymoron has to be that of *vacation stress*. How can the words "vacation" and "stress" even be put together? Simple. Whereas vacations in other parts of the world means just that—time off to relax and rest, in consumerist American culture vacations are yet another money-spending, stress spree.

Holidays on Exchange

Holiday-makers around the world are facing up to the fact that, in times of recession, large recreational expenses are difficult to justify. While to some this might seem like the end of life as they knew it, for nature lovers and ecoconscious tourists, it has prompted the discovery of some unique alternatives. Camping, hiking, cross-country skiing, bicycling, whitewater kayaking, and spelunking are all back on the radar. So is home swapping, where families trade places to reduce vacation costs.

Over the years, I have spent time in every major city in Europe through creative networking. Since my interest in sustainable living landed me residency in two ecologically desirable recreation areas—Vermont and Mount Shasta, California—doing house swaps has been easy. There are tons of services that help people make good matches, but I always just use my professional networks.

I've done dozens of house exchanges with horse lovers and philosophers from all over Europe. They've loved coming to eco-destinations in America while I've enjoyed the culture and bustle of their Continental cities. I've browsed their museums and they've hiked in my mountains. I've stayed in Cambridge, England in exchange for serving on an advisory board to a philosophical society; Amsterdam in exchange for horse-sitting de Hollandsche Manege; Lisbon, Portugal in exchange for referrals sent to a classical riding school in the area; and Florence, Italy in exchange for speaking at a philosophy conference.

It takes a little more planning than an ordinary vacation, but the results are well worth it. And, if the swap is mutually beneficial, both parties are generally open to doing it again . . . sustainable vacation! I shared the idea, several years ago, of house swaps with a colleague. At that time, he thought that it involved too much legwork to arrange and preferred, instead, to just put his vacation on his credit card.

We both spent a month in different parts of Europe that summer. When we returned to the United States and shared notes about our respective vacations, I learned that his had cost six thousand dollars. Mine had been less than half of what he had spent. I had spent a month in Amsterdam, on a writing holiday, in a gorgeous apartment directly overlooking Vondelpark. My living room looked down into the park where I watched cyclists and sunbathers enjoy a natural oasis in the middle of one of Europe's busiest cities. I worked on my writing in the mornings while eating breakfast in outdoor cafés alongside the canals. In the afternoons and evenings, I took in museums, art galleries, concerts, world cuisine, festivals, horseback riding, and lectures.

My exchange family had just as much fun at my place in Mount Shasta. They hiked on the mountain, swam in the alpine lakes, shot whitewater rapids on the rivers, bicycled, rode my horses, and enjoyed the small town farmer's markets. They cut fresh greens from my garden and ate salads outside as they watched the sun set over the surrounding mountains. We all want to do it again and, as an additional benefit, we have become friends—extended family: concentric circles of the tribe.

Recreation doesn't have to be a full-on vacation either. Recreation can be woven into the very fabric of our lives if we get creative. We just have to move it up to being a priority. I love bicycling. I live outside of the village, and whenever I have to go into town for errands, I cycle. I've equipped my bike with a large, durable basket for carrying supplies back to the Hermitage. If I have a lot of things to pick up, I wear a backpack, as well. The ride is exhilarating. By the time I've run all of my errands and ridden roundtrip, I've pedaled about ten miles. The route has some downhill parts where I am just cruising. With my sleeves rolled up, the sun penetrates my arms and my ponytail flies out behind me. I am a kid again! The climbs get my heart and lungs pumping and the endorphins release. I feel great! In those moments, all is well with the world. The sense of well-being that I experience is rejuvenating—refreshing. I re-create myself! And I run my errands at the same time: a task that could, otherwise, be a boring chore is suddenly woven into the fabric of recreation—and it's fun!

Part of our diet, back on the farm, as it still is now at the Hermitage, was made up of wildcrafted foods—foods gathered from the wild. I enjoy foraging for berries, apples and pears, meadow lettuces, watercress, and other wild edibles. Stomping through woods and marshes, in the late afternoon sunlight, in search of nature's bounty ignites my imagination. I feel wild! Suddenly, I am an ancient gatherer, reveling in the excitement of finding a lush, green stand of wild asparagus. Mythic consciousness comes alive. The butterflies come close and seem to approve as I reach carefully into the stand with my knife. I cut just enough for that night's meal, being mindful to leave some for other tribes' gatherers. I feel very connected to the earth, to the land, to humanity. And a sense of gratitude for the Mother's bounty is at the forefront of my consciousness.

Recreational foraging dials me into the implicit perfection of the great chain of being. I walk slowly home, harvest in hand, with a light heart and a deeper understanding of where I fit into the world. It is an active prayer. The asparagus isn't a commodity. It's part of me and I am part of it. When I eat it that evening, the meal is a ceremony of communion. Most certainly, I have re-created myself.

Experiencing Gratitude

The further we move away from nature—the more "advanced" we become—the less gratitude we experience. There is something about connecting with nature that just naturally increases gratitude. When I go recreational wildcrafting, I am so intimately aware of how much food Mother Nature offers us. Freely. In the spring, I see wild edible greens everywhere. In the fall, fruit falls from the trees by the roadsides. It is a very humbling insight.

The commercial food industry, on the other hand, has refined the science of taking cheap commodities pumped out by agribusiness and processing them into foodstuffs that are downright harmful. Food is more than mere fuel. And for food to rejuvenate and re-create us, we need a relationship with it. Stuff, wrapped in plastic, approaching its shelf life on a nonrecyclable piece of styrofoam, is no match for a brimming bowl of sun ripened blackberries, hand picked with friends.

It's not recreational for me to dash into the convenience aisle of the deli, grab some "stuff," and beat my way to the checkout. Spending a few hours in the countryside, though, eating one berry for every three that I drop into my basket—well, that's recreational. In both instances, I get something to eat. But only in the latter do I also re-create myself.

When my daughter turned sixteen, she wanted to have a huge Sweet Sixteen party on the farm. We all put our heads together and, after some weeks of refining our brainstorm process, came up with a party plan. Jec gave it the stamp of approval and we began putting together a party that, to this day, we all gratefully remember. We all had *so* much *fun!* We converted the indoor riding arena into a carnival. We hung Chinese lanterns, streamers, balloons, and disco balls. Then we positioned makeshift game booths all around the periphery of the arena. In this homemade midway, we set up dart games, tarot readers, balloon tying contests, ring the bottle competitions, and all sorts of other carnival games.

We had designed and produced our own funny money, with a picture of Jec in the middle—which we called "Jeccy Bucks"—for all of the party attendees to use with the various games and events. As they came into the arena, everyone got a big fistful of Jeccy Bucks they could use in the game and food booths.

In the center of the arena, we had various events happening simultaneously—bobbing for apples, watermelon eating contests, and, throughout the whole festival, a jolly clown dressed in wild polka-dotted, billowing yellow overalls with huge—massive—oversized, bright red shoes. His face was painted brilliant white with a bulbous red nose, and he had large freckles and a shock of unruly tufts of curly hair around his ears. Grinning like the Cheshire Cat, he served as a roving centerpiece to the whole event.

There was just as much activity going on outside the arena as there was inside. We had greased one of our older sows and staged a pig-riding contest. She squealed and wiggled as each youngster tried to get aboard. The winning time was a slippery sixteen-second ride. One of our quiet, older mares had been pressed into service to give pony rides. She had colored ribbons in her mane and tail and glitter on her hooves. She tiptoed along gingerly as she gave a long line of teenagers their first experience on the back of a horse.

We were careful to keep the flamboyant stilt walker away from the pony rides, so the old mare wouldn't spook or shy, and risk unseating her tenuous passengers. In the shade of a big plum tree, a magician performed sleight of hand for a fascinated audience, while a stationery mime created curiosity among the very young. The lawn of the farmhouse had morphed into a carnival kitchen, and food was passed through the windows of improvised booths: caramel apples; organic burgers on farm-baked, whole grain buns; potato salad and baked beans; sun-dried zucchini chips; gallons of spiced, fresh cider; and, of course, birthday cake and ice cream. Then, as the afternoon sun began to sink in the west, we lit the tiki torches and broke out our instruments. We danced, barefoot in the grass, as day turned into night.

It was an event that we'll all remember for the rest of our lives. It was extravagant—but not expensive. Our farm family, as well as our supportive concentric circles of friends, all pitched in to make it happen. Some of us became clowns, magicians, mimes, and puppeteers. Others barked in the game booths. A host of friends helped prepare and serve heaping platters of food. We all worked for days to get the carnival ready—days when Jec was the hub of a wheel of love. It was an event that put people first and spending second. From start to finish—setup to cleanup—the difference between *recreation* and *amusement* was blatantly obvious.

Recreation versus Amusement

Americans tend to think of the two terms interchangeably, but there are actually some significant differences. In looking at the word *amuse* etymologically, the Latin prefix *a-* means "to negate" or "not"—to negate the muses—to deny the sources of inspiration. Some translations of the Latin term *muser* go as far as to say "to stare stupidly." TV comes to mind. According to the A. C. Nielsen Co., the average American watches more than four hours of TV each day. That translates into twenty-eight hours per week, or two months of nonstop TV-watching per year. In a sixty-five-year life, the average person will have spent nine years "staring stupidly" at the tube.

Ninety-nine percent of American households possess at least one television with the average household having 2.24 TV sets. Sixty-six percent of American homes have three or more TV sets with one or another of them being on for an average of 6 hours and 47 minutes daily. Forty-nine percent of Americans feel that they watch too much TV. Nielson reports that parents spend an average of 3.5 minutes per week in meaningful conversation with their children, while their children spend an average of 1,680 minutes per week watching television. Those same children spend an average of 900 hours per year in school and an average of 1,500 hours per year watching TV, which translates into 20,000 30-second commercials a year.

There was never a TV on the farm, nor do we have one now, at the Hermitage. Kealey and I combined our books to build a personal library of over 10,000 titles. Those books have taken us on countless magic carpet rides—inward and outward—as they have kindled our imaginations and creativity. A recent National Endowment for the Arts report concluded that Americans are reading less. Their study, "To Read or Not to Read," found that an increasing number of adult Americans were not even reading one book a year.

Money spent on books, adjusted for inflation, dropped 14 percent from 1985 to 2005 and has continued to fall dramatically since the mid-1990s. Whereas we tend to think of illiteracy as primarily a third world problem, America appears to be leading the way in aliteracy— being able to read but not being interested in doing so.

While recreation is a cornerstone of the Good Life, amusement may have an eroding effect. The distinction between the two is critical. Recreation is Dionysian—rooted in nature and community, offering a fulcrum point between duty and freedom. It refreshes, rejuvenates, and revitalizes us. The Good Life is a life lived in balance between what we *must* do and what we *can* do.

A Dozen Things You Can Do

- Make sure that you use all of your accrued annual vacation time. View it as an investment in your health and well-being.
- Get familiar with the Take Back Your Time national initiative. They have recently launched a YouTube channel that has many good videos on the importance of vacation. Educate yourself!
- Clarify the distinction between *recreation* and *amusement*. Try to envision ways that you and your family could move more toward recreation and less toward amusement.
- Research possibilities for setting up vacation exchanges with other individuals or families. Think international! This a really topflight way to learn about other cultures.
- Weave recreation into the fabric of your life. Envision ways to have "home vacations" where you intermingle daily responsibilities with recreation. If you are a teacher, you might, for example, grade assignments by the side of a lake—taking a swim about midway through the task.
- Brainstorm a list of recreational ideas that you and your family or friends can enjoy together that cost nothing. Look in the community calendar section of your local paper to find out about free events in your area: concerts, festivals, art walks, lectures, and films are often offered for free.
- Check out your local libraries' inventory of audio books. These make great companions—stimulating your intellect—while exercising, traveling, or doing housework.
- Collect and press wildflowers that you can later use to make gorgeous, original collages for special gifts. Store them pressed flat between multiple sheets of old newspaper in a dark, dry drawer.
- Try Laughter Yoga. Our true nature is playful. Yet life often causes us to become overly serious. Then we squish our joy inside of us instead of expressing it freely. Go ahead: laugh for no reason!

- Learn to play—really play. Do things that have no "value"—other than that you like to do them—attached to them. Give yourself the gift of playing.
- Support legislation and initiatives that are pro-vacation.
- Practice gratitude. Learn to appreciate the simple, substantive things in life. Saying "thank you" (often) is both free and freeing.

9

Halfway Up the Mountain

Knowing is not enough; we must apply.
Willing is not enough; we must do.

—Johann Wolfgang von Goethe

The gift of Dionysus is utter freedom. This is in contrast to Apollo, whose gift is order. When in the ecstatic grip of Dionysus's magic, we find nothing impossible. When Dionysus arrives, Apollo's well-ordered world is shattered. A tempest of creative energy is unleashed and traditional mores lose their power to bind. The poor feel rich; the slave, free. Apollo applauds conformity; Dionysus beckons us outside the box.

Apollo and Dionysus, as states of mind, entered Western consciousness as members of the twelve Olympians—the principal gods of the Greek pantheon, residing on Mount Olympus. Apollo became identified with the principle of individuation, self-control, perfection, rationality, and logic. Dionysus, on the other hand, represented instinct, intuition, wholeness, and the celebration of nature.

In a contemporary sense, we might call Apollo the left brain and Dionysus, the right. Thus, Apollo beckons us to our minds, while Dionysus reminds us of our hearts. Everything that is part of our unique individuality is Apollonian. Enthusiasm and ecstasy are Dionysian, for in these states we give up our individuality and merge with the greater whole.

The Engineering of Consent

Americans emerged from World War II with the terrifying realization that the human race could self-destruct. The tremendous, irrational, malignant power that emerged during the war had demonstrated that mankind was, indeed, capable of annihilation. Consequently, the whole concept of rationality, the Apollonian, and irrationality, the Dionysian, was called into question with many important cultural voices seeing the question from different perspectives.

Freud, powerlessly hemmed in between two World Wars, posited that the Holocaust had been a demonstrative culmination of unchecked irrational forces that had incrementally bubbled up from beneath the surface of humanity's conscious mind.

Freud's daughter, Anna, in conjunction with her cousin Edward Bernays, both highly influential forces in America during the 1950s, put a pragmatic spin on the elder Freud's classical work and emphasized the importance of the ego: the constant struggle and conflict that it experiences by the need to answer contradicting wishes, desires, values, and demands of reality.

Anna Freud's psychoanalytic work with children convinced her that people could be trained to conform to the expectations of society—to buy into the dominant social standards of their culture. By the late 1950s, psychoanalysis had become the prime force driving consumerism in America. Most corporations hired public relations specialists, otherwise known as "spin doctors," who followed Bernays' model of exploiting subconscious drives that ignited consumer interest.

The ideas of Anna Freud and Edward Bernays were so influential, in fact, on American social development in the 1950s that they implemented, without any public resistance, what they called the "engineering of consent." Americans, under the influence of this social engineering, consented to become Ozzie and Harriet. We dressed alike, thought alike, and bought alike! The left-brained Apollo was appeased and the American social fabric was orderly, tidy, and predictable.

The pendulum, though, invariably swings. And, as the 1950s morphed into the 1960s, new voices opposed the Freudian idea of repressing the inner self in the interest of engineering conformity. These new psychologists thought that the self should be allowed to express itself. They believed that out of this philosophy would come a new type of strong human being and a better society.

This ideology, known as the human potential movement, culminated at Esalen Institute under the direction of Dr. Fritz Perls, who sought to liberate people's hitherto repressed feelings so they could live intensely emotional lives. Dionysus danced around his throne as Americans threw off the shackles of conformity and began to seek their unique individuality.

While the Freudian school of the 1950s—dominated by the idea that human beings were driven by irrational, unconscious instincts—believed that it was society's job to repress these instincts, the human growth movement of the 1960s felt that the unconscious forces inside the human mind were legitimate and had only become distorted through their repression by society.

Herbert Marcuse[1] was an important voice in this psychosocial shift. In *One Dimensional Man,* Marcuse claimed that Freudian psychology had helped to create a world in which people were reduced to expressing their feelings and identities through mass-produced objects: "stuff." The Freudian influence had burnt offerings to Apollo while the human growth movement bowed to Dionysus.

In truth, however, we aren't going to self-actualize if we are only using half of our capacity. If we are swayed to worship Apollo and our left brains are lit up and supercharged, that means that Dionysus, or our right brain, is dozing. When Dionysus naps, we are neither creative nor compassionate. The same is true conversely. If Dionysus is at the helm without the hand of Apollo also on the wheel, we may be emotionally fluent and intuitive, but we aren't as plugged in analytically as we need to be to steer the course. We need to make room in our psyches for these two gods to walk side by side.

That means that we have to embrace the tension of opposites—

something that Americans, who crave certainty and comfort, aren't all that good at. Embracing the opposites requires resting, rather uncomfortably, in paradox. C. G. Jung articulated, quite eloquently, that when we go into our psyches, we are invariably going to meet the problem of the opposites.

This is the very double bind that is at the root of our own self-consciousness. Jung reminded us that holding to the tension of opposites can be an excruciating experience. It requires the death of the neurotic ego. In Jung's own words, "the birth of the Self is always a defeat for the ego." We are only able to creatively hold to the tension of the opposites if we realize that the opposites themselves are manifestations of the Self and not of the ego.[2] This means worshipping both Apollo and Dionysus simultaneously—using cognition and emotion in concert. Cultivating exterior experience based on interior knowledge.

Bring Back Dionysus

Marcuse gave us a glimpse of this potential when he wrote, "Education today must involve the mind and the body, reason and imagination, the intellectual and the instinctual needs."[3] Marcuse's statement reflects the admiration of the Frankfurt School, with which he was affiliated, for Nietzsche.[4]

Nietzsche had realized that life was not governed by solely rational principles. There are no absolute standards of good and evil that can be demonstrated by human reason. Nietzsche railed against industrial, bourgeois society—which we would call *consumer culture*—thinking that it made man decadent and feeble because it made him a victim of the excessive development of the rational faculties at the expense of human will and instinct. In other words, that humans are disempowered by the segregated Apollonian.

Were Nietzsche here today, he would caution us against the tendencies of consumer culture, urging us, instead, to recognize the dark and mysterious world of instinct, which he considered to be the true life force. He would shake his finger at us and probably even raise his voice as he reminded us that *excessive* rationality, an *over-reliance* on human reason, does little more than smother the spontaneity necessary for creativity. For us to realize our potential, he would say, we must sever our singular over-dependence on the Apollonian and, instead, beckon Dionysus back to the table. Offering a counterposition to psychosocial Freudianism, Nietzsche—through Marcuse—invites us to reintegrate the right brain.

Marcuse's "one dimensional man" is Apollonian, representing the force of the established order, the mass culture. Apollo assumes a conformity that rewards exteriority. Who we are in the world is determined by what we have—our "stuff." Americans, unwittingly, *become* their homes, cars, portfolios, and titles. Their inner compass sits on the shelf as outer maps are forged and followed.

Career paths, financial success, and social status trump family, recreation, and spirituality. Nature becomes something that is visited on an occasional weekend, rather than a system in which we are nested. Exteriorized Americans, like the White Rabbit, race against the clock, dashing from thing to thing desperately seeking satisfaction "out there," somewhere.

Values and Lifestyles

The Stanford Research Institute (SRI) Values and Lifestyles Survey (VALS) has determined that 67 percent of the American population is outer-directed, while only 20 percent is inner-directed. Of even greater concern is that only 2 percent are what the survey calls outer- and inner-directed, or integrated.[43]

Inner-directeds contrast with outer-directeds in that they conduct their lives primarily in accord with inner values. These are people who do not feel defined by their places in society, or by what they own, but by the choices they can make for themselves. They are more interested in what is "in here" than what is "out there."

Concern with inner growth is a cardinal characteristic. It is important to recognize that, in contemporary American society, one can hardly be profoundly inner-directed without having internalized outer-directedness through extensive and deep prior exposure. Some measure of satiation with exteriority seems to be required before a person can believe in or enjoy the less material, incorporeal values of inner direction.

From a psychological standpoint, the shift to inner direction represents an advance over outer direction in that it adds new values to old, thus increasing the range of potential responses and the number of channels available for self-expression. Taking the inward journey, exploring ourselves as if we are labyrinths, reconnects us with right brain, or Dionysian, potentialities.

According to Daniel Pink, author of *A Whole New Mind: Why Right-Brainers Will Rule the Future*, writes that the era of left-brain dominance and the Information Age that it engendered is giving way to a new world in which right-brain qualities, such as empathy and meaning, will predominate. The Agricultural and Industrial Ages have come and gone and the Information Age is fading fast. We're hurtling into a Conceptual Age where, according to Pink, empathy is an asset above logic; play, above seriousness; and meaning, above accumulation. Pink's vision of right-brainers, or inner-directeds, stepping up to bat in the incoming Conceptual Age has some exciting implications, not the least of which would include a cultural shift from consumerist "goods lives" to more meaningful "Good lives."

Turning Inside Out

I arrived at the farm a fully enculturated, exteriorized person. I had just clawed my way through graduate school and was in the process of deciding who I would be in the world. My eyes were on things "out there." In retrospect, I can see that even the farm's mission statement appealed to my sense of exteriority. I wanted to change the world: to help build a society that was ecologically aware and life sustaining.

Little did I know that those twenty-two years would turn me, literally, inside out. The farm was like a living labyrinth. Carl Jung, in a letter to Karl Kerenyi, wrote, "the labyrinth is indeed a primordial image which one encounters as . . . a descent into the underworld."[6] It is the topography of the unconscious. The labyrinth combines the imagery of the circle and the spiral into a meandering, but purposeful, path representing a journey to our own center and back again out into the world. It offers only one way: unicursal. The way in is the way out. But the person who comes out is not the same as the person who went in. Moving our focus from ego identification toward connection with the true self—our authenticity—the labyrinth boots up the right brain's Dionysian sense of inner direction.

Long, dark Vermont winter nights; caring for animals; tending gardens; raising children; preserving food; stacking firewood; handcrafting gifts; playing instruments; drawing and painting, and living in community, all began to turn my eyes toward things "in there."

Putting one foot in front of the next, I walked incrementally smaller concentric circles, spiraling in toward my own center. With every turn of the spiral, I got one step closer to answering the quintessential philosophical question, "Who am I?" while simultaneously realizing that I may never know. Sometimes it was excruciating and, other times, liberating.

The tension of opposites became more than something merely theoretical. I remember long nights of playing my harpsichord against the backdrop of howling winter winds. As night temperatures dropped below zero and snow pelted against the windows, the old farmhouse would get so cold that I would wrap myself in a comforter to play my beloved baroque music. More often than not, the storm knocked out the electricity, leaving me to play by the flickering light of an antique oil lamp. The children, tucked snugly in their beds, loved to hear the plectra produce Telemann, Couperin, and Scarlatti. They called it "falling asleep to the sound of the tinkling strings."

But, for me, it was a whole lot more. It was Apollo and Dionysus's challenge for me to reconcile cognition and emotion.

The Übermensch

It was on one of those nights that I began to really get inside Nietzsche's head and wrap my mind around his concept of the Übermensch.[7] Buried beneath layers of speculative—and even perverted—political interpretation, I could see that Nietzsche's Superman had gotten lost. Then, suddenly, there he stood, suspended between Apollo and Dionysus.

As I engaged in the exterior, technical aspects of playing the harpsichord, the music prompted an interior, emotional response. Contrary to Nietzsche's "last man" who only desired personal immediate gratification, or Marcuse's "one dimensional man" who was simply a composite of his stuff, the Übermensch lived a life of meaning and purpose: a Good Life.

Most Americans are part of the outer-directed, materialistic, consumer herd: one dimensional last men. The Übermensch, on the other hand—the mere 2 percent of the American population that integrates outer and inner direction—has begun the trek up Mount Olympus. It's the road less traveled by, where heart is valued as much as head; music as much as logic; and nature as much as commerce. It takes courage to take the first few faltering steps. Or does it?

A Dozen Things You Can Do

- Build a labyrinth in your yard. This can be a very simple construction, made out of rocks or sticks. Walk it, both inwardly and outwardly, meditatively every day for thirty days. Note whether or not you experienced any inner shifts.

- Listen to music that is specially created to affect brain hemisphere synchronization. Programs such as EquiSync, Holosync, Hemi-Sync, or other binaural audio programs, create new neural pathways between the left and right hemispheres, balancing the brain. Through this process fear, phobias, anxiety, worry, and chronic pain begin to dissipate.

- Designate one day each week as a day when you will not use your cell phone, laptop, or handheld.

- Take a free online test to determine your brain hemisphere dominance. There are many very good versions of these tests available on the Internet. Are you right or left brain–dominant? What does this mean for you?

- Watch Adam Curtis's award-winning 2002 BBC documentary, *The Century of the Self*. It is available for free download and streaming on the Internet.

- Take a community qigong class and explore the relationship between balancing the body and balancing the brain.

- Attempt a multiple day silent meditation retreat. Journal what comes up for you as you work with the Silence.

- Get a yoga professional to teach you some inversion asanas, which help create blood flow to the head, thereby creating more brain health. Many people report greater hemispheric synchronization after practicing inversion.

- Balance your brain and body by listening to high frequency classical music at least once a day. Any sound between 5,000 and 8,000 hertz has been found to recharge our brain's batteries.

- If you are right-handed, try being left-handed for a day—and vice versa. Make a note of any cognitive or perceptual changes that you discover.

- Sample Eye Movement Desensitization and Reprocessing, or EMDR, therapy. The EMDR therapy uses bilateral stimulation, right/left eye movement, which repeatedly activates the opposite sides of the brain, thereby assisting the mind–body connection.
- Try, with a qualified practitioner, a neurofeedback (EEG biofeedback) session, which enables a person to alter their brainwaves. Journal the experience. What did you discover when your brainwaves were altered?

10

The Wisdom of Insecurity

*But the attitude of faith is to let go, and become open
to truth, whatever it might turn out to be.*

—Alan Watts

A recent guest, after a few days in residence at my California Hermitage, commented, "You have worked out a *really* fabulous life for yourself—but it must have taken courage." She had been hard-hit by the recent economic downturn and was thinking about making some changes in her life. But she was scared. She valued security. Up until the recent turn of events, Carmen had seen "the system" as secure. So secure, in fact, that she had never really even questioned it. Affluenza had kept her unconscious, lulling her to sleep. But the economic crisis had been a wake-up call. Now she was taking a long, hard look at her lifestyle. Was it sustainable? Could she sustain her consumer habits? Did she even want to? What was the stress of time poverty doing to her health? Layoffs at her workplace, downsizing in her professional field, and a devalued retirement portfolio all pointed to how illusory the "security" of conventional culture was. The recession had not only left its mark on Carmen's bank account, but also on her mind.

A recent international poll, conducted by *Reader's Digest,* asked people from sixteen countries one simple question: What stresses you the most? A total of one-hundred-fifty participants from each country chose between money, family, their health, or the state of the world. The results showed that most participants, like Carmen, considered money to be the number one reason for stress. Malaysia led the list with 58 percent of participants stating money to be their biggest concern, followed by China and Singapore with both 55 percent. Third in the list was the United States, with 48 percent of participants blaming the declining dollar for their stress. On the other hand, nations reporting the least concern about money were Russia, France, and Italy. In Russia, only 15 percent said they were stressed about money, while in France and Italy the number was 18 and 19 percent respectively. Most participants from these three countries said their concerns centered more on their family than on money. Does it take courage to put family before money—or wisdom?

Jean Paul Getty, founder of Getty Oil and inarguably one of the richest Americans to ever live, is a striking example of putting money before family. Often working sixteen to eighteen hours a day to handle the complex transactions of his multifarious business dealings, Getty wrote in 1965 that he couldn't "remember a single day of vacation in the last 45 years that was not somehow interrupted by a cable, telegram or telephone call that made me tend to business for at least a few hours." Admitting that his self-imposed work schedule had taken a heavy toll on his personal life, his family life was in shambles.

Five failed marriages were the least of it. The most potent example of his valuing money over family is found in his response to the 1973 kidnapping of his sixteen-year-old grandson, John Paul Getty III. On July 10, 1973 in Rome, sixteen-year-old John Paul Getty III was kidnapped and a ransom of $17 million was demanded for his safe return. When Jean Paul Getty's son asked his father for the money, the senior Getty flatly refused. In November of the same year an envelope containing a lock of hair and a human ear was delivered to a daily newspaper, with a threat of further mutilation unless $3.2 million was paid. The message read, "This is Paul's ear. If we don't get some money within 10 days, then the other ear will arrive. In other words, he will arrive in little bits."

At this juncture, J. Paul Getty agreed to pay a ransom that he, however, negotiated down to $2 million and required his son, Paul II, to repay the amount in full at 4% interest.

One of the most insidious examples of how money has preempted family can be found in the increase in family labor hours over the past few decades. According to the Bureau of Labor Statistics, more than 60 percent of families with children under age 18 had both parents employed outside the home in 2005–2006. That figure has doubled since 1975. In 1970, the one-income family saved 11 percent of its take-home pay and allocated 1.4 percent of its annual income to pay revolving debt, such as credit cards. In 2005, the two-income family saved nothing, and allocated 15 percent of its annual income to revolving debt.

Statistics indicate that when both partners work full-time, families spend more, consume more, borrow more, and save less than when only one partner works full-time or both partners work part-time. According to a new Pew Research Center survey, only one-in-five, or 21 percent, of mothers with minor children report that full-time work is an ideal situation for them. This figure is down from the 32 percent who reported this back in 1997. Fully six-in-ten of today's working mothers report that part-time work would be their ideal. This number is up from the 48 percent reported in 1997.

Working to Live versus Living to Work

Do we *work to live* or *live to work?* That question loomed large at the start of the Great Depression, as W. K. Kellogg launched his revolutionary six-hour workday. Kellogg Management, propelled by a vision of Liberation Capitalism, insisted that six-hour workdays would revolutionize society by shifting the balance of time from economic concerns to the challenge of freedom.

As World War II drew to a close, though, full-time work was propagandized. Personal discretionary time was trivialized and shorter work hours were feminized. The message was that only sissies, misfits, and "girls" who "didn't even know enough" to realize the importance of a full-time job would be interested in part-time work.

This kind of thinking still hangs on today. While the Pew Research Center Survey found that six-in-ten working mothers would love to have part-time employment, they did not find the same to be true of working males. Part-time work is much less popular among contemporary fathers, according to the Pew Survey, with about seven-in-ten, or 72 percent of men with minor age children, reporting that full-time work is their ideal situation.

Contemporary social conditioning strongly suggests that if a person doesn't work full-time—especially men—they are a loser. Men who are out of full-time work, even though it may be one of the most potent times of their lives, feel "less than" in the eyes of their peers. The pervasive, dominant cultural myth indicates that working full-time is a straight shot to *security:* through income, insurance, and retirement benefits. But, as Carmen had discovered, the myth has some holes in it.

One of the things that I learned on the farm was the value of having free time, during which I chose activities that gave meaning and purpose to my day. I noticed that people who worked at full-time jobs, and tried to pursue other interests and responsibilities, were quite stressed out. I decided, early on, that I wasn't willing to put aside my creative interests in deference to work. So the farm's policy of part-time work appealed to me. My dual professional interests of dressage and philosophy fit hand-in-glove as part-time work. During the academic year, I taught philosophy part-time at an area university and, likewise, taught dressage part-time during semester breaks and summers.

My well-intentioned friends advised me about not being able to make an adequate living or retire well without the security of full-time work. But I figured that I hadn't moved to a back-to-the-earth commune in Vermont in search of security. Let's face it, we were trying to grow all of our own food and the New England climate sometimes provided as few as one hundred frost-free days in a year. There wasn't much security looking me in the face.

I felt more like one of Jacques Rancière's[1] worker-poets, viewing the free time as a longed-for oasis. I saw my discretionary time as outside of the stress, struggle, and conflict of a workplace. In it, there were no frictions of class, gender, control, necessity, or structure. I had stepped outside of what Josef Pieper[2] called the modern "world of total work." Pieper reminded me of Aristotle's rather startling assertion that "the first principle of action is leisure."

But Pieper also pointed out that I needed to be clear about the distinction between *leisure* and *idleness*.[3] Leisure, unlike mere idleness, refers to our contemplative selves, to our ability to passively receive knowledge and wisdom. Leisure is not simply a lack of work. It, rather, reflects a spiritual viewpoint from which we can accept that there are priorities greater than the ones we set for ourselves.

Some of the priorities that were greater than the ones that I might have set for myself included mastering a highly personalized and creative painting technique that helped me achieve an artistic style that is truly my own; learning to finger mordents and other baroque keyboard ornaments flawlessly; and becoming fluent in two foreign languages. In Victor Turner's[4] words, I found "an independent domain of creative activity" that was outside of universal utilitarianism that sought to turn everything into some useful purpose.[5] How could I weigh the satisfaction of these priorities against the security of "the system"? Should I have chosen the more secure route instead, of working full-time in order to fund a retirement account?

Recent economic events have indicated that there was actually a kind of wisdom in the insecurity that I chose.

Retirement Options

The 2008 market wipeout showed the vulnerability of popular retirement savings accounts. Anyone who has even peeked at their account statements following that event realizes that there is something painfully wrong with the system. From the end of 2007 to the end of

March 2009, the average 401(k) balance fell 31 percent, according to Fidelity. In a system where one year's gains build on the next, disasters like the one that occurred in 2008 will dent retirement options long after any downturn ends.

The Society for Professional Asset Managers and Record Keepers says nearly 73 million Americans, or just under 50 percent of the U.S. working population, have a 401(k). Collectively, those millions of Americans pour more than $200 billion into these accounts each year. The average 401(k) account balance, however, is only $45,519 and 46 percent of all 401(k) accounts have less than $10,000.

Alicia Munnell, who heads the Center for Retirement Research at Boston College, advises that 401(k)s should not be the principle thing upon which Americans rely for retirement security. Even the U.S. government agrees. The Government Accountability Office recently concluded that "if no action is taken, a considerable number of Americans face the prospect of a reduced standard of living in retirement."

The idea that we could ever save enough to pay for thirty or so years of retirement is a relatively recent invention. An entire profession, financial planning, is dedicated to telling people that they can pay for their retirements through 401(k)s or other similar instruments. But, by Munnell's calculations, 44 percent of all Americans are in danger of going broke in the post-work years. And, according to conventional wisdom, this is the end result of a "secure" system!

Conventional wisdom suggests working full-time and contributing heftily to one's retirement portfolio. This is generally referred to as a part of the "benefits" package associated with full-time work. Security? Remember that the biggest factor associated with whether or not your plan pans out has to do with *when* you retire. If the market rises during that year, you're fine. If, though, you retired after a crash, you're toast.

The market fell in four of the nine years since the beginning of the decade. That means that anyone retiring this decade had a nearly 50 percent chance of leaving work in a down market. Right now, your chances of retiring into a down market are even greater than that, since forced retirements spike in recessions, just as the stock market is tanking.

Nonetheless, the prevailing wisdom still claims that if you are currently making $50,000 a year, you need to have no less than a half-million dollars in investments and retirement funds in order to maintain your lifestyle upon retirement. These calculations are based on a formula that states your investments have to generate the equivalent of at least 80 percent of your preretirement income.

This all comes apart, however, if you decide that you don't want to "maintain your lifestyle." What if, for example, you prefer to cash out on your suburban lifestyle and move out to the country where you can learn to live sustainably and move toward being as self-sufficient as possible? Then, the formula is different. For every $100 you cut your retirement monthly cost of living, that is $15,000 less—yes, fifteen thousand dollars less!—that you have to have in your retirement savings plan. The math goes like this: if your investments earn 8 percent annually, then $15,000 will generate $1200 a year, or $100 a month. So if you don't need that $100 a month, you then save yourself having to put away that $15,000.

It's pretty easy to shave $100 a month off of the bills of a sustainable lifestyle with some solid planning. Solar panels, wind generators, and an environmentally friendly woodstove reduce utility bills to almost nothing. It's also amazing how far your money will go when you don't have a mortgage, car payments, or credit card debt. Put in a garden and formerly scary grocery costs become a thing of the past. It's not about "maintaining your lifestyle." It's about creating a *new* lifestyle—a sustainable, voluntarily simple Good Life.

Of course, there is always the alternative option of simply working longer. Put retirement on the back burner and just keep your nose to the grindstone. That doesn't sound like a recipe for the Good Life to me. Nor does it sound like there is much wisdom in the "security" of conventional work life.

What if, instead of working full-time and investing earned income into risky financial products, people chose to work part-time and invest the earned time into things that would contribute to a more

comfortable retirement further down the road? Part-time work schedules create less temporal stress than do full-time schedules. Part-time
workers have sufficient time to manage household chores, care for
children, do errands, and meet social obligations without "burning the
candle at both ends." So people who are less stressed-out—not running
around for years like Mad Hatters—have less health problems.

Part-time workers who approach retirement without stress-related
degenerative diseases, not requiring expensive medications and medical procedures, have achieved a sustainable alternative to the all too
prevalent debilitation of the average American retiree.

Working Full-Time Reconsidered

The National Institute for Occupational Safety and Health and the
American Psychological Association report that full-time working
conditions have overburdened American's traditional coping mecha-
nisms. The inability to balance obligations between incrementally
more demanding full-time work and family life has exploded.

Demands for increased productivity and longer work hours have
contributed to growing psychological tensions. Globally, 23 percent
of full-time female professionals, and 19 percent of their male peers,
report feeling "super-stressed." A 2006 study published by the Migra-
tion Policy Institute reported that the number of visas issued to U.S.
retirees in Panama tripled between 2003 and 2005 and the number
of U.S. retirees to some regions of Mexico jumped by nearly 200
percent. The reason? Affordable health costs.

Chronic diseases that begin to show up as early as forty years of
age are exacerbated by age sixty: hypertension, heart problems, irritable bowel, and diabetes—all long-term, stress-related conditions.
According to the National Committee to Preserve Social Security and
Medicare, the average senior takes between six and eight different
prescription drugs a day. One in five retirees, according to the Kaiser
Family Foundation, reports managing the costs of these prescriptions
by cutting back on other basic necessities. Security?

A young man lived at the farm for several years who used to tell us that we should work our dressage horses much less strenuously. He said, "a horse only has so many steps in it and you want each of those steps to count." He had the same idea about the dairy cows. He felt that they should all be asked to produce a bit less milk and not have so much strain put upon their reproductive systems. His advice seemed sound, so we employed it.

Soon after we made some of his suggested modifications, the farm equine vet commented to me that if all dressage riders managed their horses the way that I did, she would be out of business. My horses' sports injuries and stress-related disorders had dropped off the radar. They were happy, performing at the top of their game, and in radiant health. The same was true of our dairy cows. We reduced the pressure for them to produce, and let them make milk more naturally, according to their own individual rhythms. We noticed that they stayed sleeker and shinier, were more contented, and had greater longevity. And we still got plenty of milk for the farmhouse. Our horses and cows became part-time workers, excelling in their respective professions without paying the high price of stress-induced, compromised health.

Alternative Retirement Options

One of the most sustainable course corrections that I made was redirecting monies earmarked for retirement away from volatile financial products and toward what I prefer to call sustainable lifestyle products: a greenhouse, solar panels, water conservation systems, alternative transportation, and cohousing options. Let's look at this in terms of dollars and cents. The 2009 solo 401(k) salary elective deferral limit was $16,500. The corresponding IRA annual limit was between $5,000 and $6,000, depending on the depositor's age. According to the Consumer Price Index, the current inflation rate is minus 1.3 percent, which means that we are technically in a period of deflation.[6]

Deflation occurs when asset and consumer prices spiral downward in response to a long-term drop in demand. Unfortunately, the current drop in demand triggering deflation is due to job losses, declining wages, and ongoing declines in real estate and portfolio values. So monies dumped into investment homes, 401(k)s, IRAs and other financial instruments over the years have, instead of providing secure nest eggs for retirement, actually lost value.

I recently took the same amount of money that I could have contributed to a 401(k) and IRA and, instead, put it into a cohousing option that is reaping benefits not contingent upon the ups and downs of an unstable financial market. By reclaiming some previously wasted space in the Hermitage, we opened up additional living space that is now offered to WWOOF (World Wide Opportunities on Organic Farms) interns.

WWOOF is an international movement that is helping people share more sustainable ways of living. We provide accommodation, share our meals, and teach WWOOFers about organic gardening, composting, practical permaculture, wildcrafting, food preservation, and other aspects of simple, ecologically sound living in exchange for their volunteer help at the Hermitage. It's another win-win situation— and one in which the returns have been more satisfying than those offered by "the system."

The interns take away skills to improve the quality of their lives. Our gardens are lush and verdant, saving us thousands of dollars a year in grocery bills. And eating produce fresh from the garden has contributed to all of our radiant health. Most importantly, we're participating in a network of shared intention and sustainable community that has ramifications for building a whole new paradigm based on cooperation and reciprocity.

People who are currently laid off or furloughed, and may not have the financial resources to put toward a sustainable lifestyle project, can still put their newly acquired *time* toward similar projects. Sustainability isn't just about alternative energy projects, Energy Star appliances, hybrid cars, greeting cards made from elephant dung, or supporting the World Wildlife Federation. It can be as simple as spending time building cold frames from reclaimed materials, tending an old abandoned orchard, wildcrafting, planting a new garden, or any number of other do-it-yourself projects.

We live in a time of unprecedented insecurity. Many long-established traditions are breaking down—traditions of family and social life, of government, of the economic order, and of religious belief. As the years go by, there are fewer and fewer rocks to which we can hold.[7] We can either view this change as terrifying or we can view it as a welcome release from the restraints of old, outworn cultural structures—as an opportunity to create something new.

A Dozen Things You Can Do

- Take the Holmes-Rahe Life Stress Inventory, which is available for free online, to assess the level of stress you are experiencing in your day-to-day life. We are often so accustomed to our stressors that we don't even notice them anymore. This inventory will bring certain stress patterns to your attention.
- Calculate what you spend in order to work full-time. Expenses should include any item or service that you would not need to purchase if you had the time to make or do it yourself (for example, child-care services, meal preparation, household cleaning, yard work, home maintenance, etc.).
- Conversely, calculate what you could save by working part-time.
- Identify a hobby that you really, truly enjoy ("an independent domain of creative activity") and brainstorm ways that you could turn it into a profitable part-time business.
- Set a goal of shaving $100 a month off of your bills by implementing more sustainable lifestyle practices.
- Take out your lawn and replace it with an organic vegetable garden. Plan your new garden with attention to aesthetics, as well as utility, by incorporating interesting plant groupings, floral borders, herbs, and original rock sculptures.
- Consider diversifying your professional efforts by enjoying several mini-jobs instead of one, all-consuming career.
- Create an English tea garden, using all natural materials. Plant an array of herbs that you can enjoy fresh all summer and dried throughout the rest of the year. Position an improvised little table, with a pretty coverlet, in the garden for intimate tea parties.
- Learn to brew your own kombucha tea. Serve it chilled, in frosted mugs, on hot afternoons. Try infusing it with fresh ginger, pomegranate, or lemon to create a signature flavor.
- Assess how comfortable—or not—you are with risk taking by

taking the Strong Interest Inventory. Many good, free versions of this test are available online. Do you like to "play it safe" or "take chances"?

- Do some hard math. Calculate, based on the current balance in your 401(k), how many years until you can retire. If you find the outcome of this fact-finding to be untenable, brainstorm alternative ideas about your retirement plans.

- Are you passionate about your work or are you only working for the paycheck? In the case of the latter, schedule an appointment with a life coach and see if she can help you identify some career options you may have overlooked.

11

Behaving as if All Life Matters

A man is truly ethical only when he obeys the
compulsion to help all life which he is able to assist,
and shrinks from injuring anything that lives.

—Albert Schweitzer

Relationship is the missing piece that brings sustainable lifestyles full circle. Through including interpersonal relationships in the sustainability quotient, the vision of creating something new begins to take on tangible form. Through sustainable relationship principles and practices, families and friends can better prepare for challenge and change, and through this preparation become fortified for times of insecurity. When times get tough, strong relationships can give people the courage to hold on to what works and, consequently, reduce the devastating effects of life's challenges. Sustainable relationships are the rocks to which we can hold. But twenty-first-century Americans need some reminders about how to create sustainable relationships.

Americans for Divorce Reform estimates that, if current trends continue, between 40 to 50 percent of marriages will end in divorce. Jennifer Baker of the Forest Institute of Professional Psychology in Springfield, Missouri confirms that 50 percent of first marriages are destined to end in divorce, while 67 percent of second and 74 percent of third marriages will most likely do so. America has the highest divorce rate in the world. These statistics suggest that American values have shifted from the importance of family to that of *self*-importance: people want what is good for themselves without considering if it is beneficial for others.

Consumerism has conditioned people to think in terms of obsolescence. If something doesn't work, you just get rid of it—throw it out. This attitude, unfortunately, carries over into relationships: if the marriage doesn't work, you can get a divorce. Just like it's easier to buy a new washing machine than it is to get the old one fixed, it's easier to throw in the towel than it is to put in the time and effort to make a marriage work. I am not saying that there is not a time and a place for divorce. There is. It is an option—but only one of many that have to be weighed and considered.

Rugged Individualism

Societies are organized around either individual or collective values. In individualist societies the ties between people are quite loose: everyone is only expected to look after himself and his immediate family. To the contrary, in collectivist societies, people, from the cradle to the grave, are integrated into strong, cohesive groups, including extended families.

The United States is highly individualistic, scoring 91 on the Hofstede Dimension of Culture Scale. Americans value independence and self-reliance, to the point of shunning the imposition of collective or group goals. The American Dream is a good example of this rugged individualism. The belief that everyone can pull themselves up by their bootstraps depends upon competition, one-upmanship, and an overall dog-eat-dog social ethic.

It's amazing how sentences written over one hundred-fifty years ago by Alexis de Tocqueville,[1] in *Democracy in America,* so accurately describe the mentality of the contemporary American middle class. De Tocqueville was concerned that rugged individualism would undermine America's free institutions if the citizenry withdrew into incrementally more isolated, small circles of family and friends, progressively turning their backs on larger social networks and, consequently, not participating in public structures. Tocqueville worried that our obsessive concern for material betterment and economic advancement could ultimately cost us our freedom.

Both the baby boomers and Generation X have given new meaning to individualism. These are the "me" generations. If it feels good, do it. Boomers have mortgaged their children's futures for their own personal comforts. Children are now born burdened with thousands of dollars of debt from the moment they enter the world.

There has been an underlying shift in American culture: a relentless rise of narcissism, an inflated view of self brought on by reality television, economic bubbles, and easy credit. Five times as many Americans undergo plastic surgery and cosmetic procedures as ten years ago, and ordinary people hire fake paparazzi to follow them around to make them look famous. The shift has affected us all—witness Wall Street greed and the mortgage crisis with its overblown sense of materialism and entitlement.

In *The Narcissism Epidemic: Living in the Age of Entitlement*, psychologists and professors Jean Twenge and W. Keith Campbell argue that the nation needs to recognize this social epidemic and its negative consequences, and begin to take corrective action. They recommend that individuals start by practicing gratitude, while parents teach their children friendship skills, with an emphasis on others rather than self. In other words, incorporating collectivist values.

Collectivism

Collectivism is a term used to designate the cultural trait of giving primacy to the goals and welfare of groups: to relationships with other humans. Collectivist culture is generally high context, with multiple layers of shared meanings related to historical context, social norms and roles.

I got a lot of lessons about collectivism living on the farm. Some were fraught with the angst, turmoil, and conflict of many different people exploring ways of living together. Others were maps for the potential of conscious community.

One that particularly stands out in my mind is the story of Floyd. I was in my late twenties and Floyd was in his late eighties. Floyd did horse dentistry for a living and I had a barn full of horses, so we got to know each other well. Floyd was the prototype of a Vermonter . . . hard working, generous, and honest. His wife had died some years earlier and he was alone.

One day, while he was attending to a horse in my barn, I asked him who would help him when he got old? He smiled quietly and said that he had no worries about that, because "the horse people" would be there. I remember thinking that he might be a bit naive. But I also remember hoping that he was right.

One Thanksgiving morning, in a particularly blustery Vermont snowstorm, I hitched my old black Morgan stallion to a Portland cutter sleigh and drove over to Floyd's to drop off a couple of pies. It was like pulling into a midwinter horse show. People had driven, ridden, walked, snowshoed, and skied over to his place with all sorts of delectables. Between all of us, Floyd had a rather handsome Thanksgiving dinner and good company as well.

He had been right, "the horse people" were helping him . . . bringing in firewood, mucking his stalls, and getting his wood cookstove fired up to keep the dinner warm. When the day came, some years later, for Floyd to cross over to the other side, we were all there to help him. I had learned the essence of community from this old-timer. We took shifts to care for him and his horses, ran errands, chipped in to keep his electricity paid, and just generally did what an extended family would do to make a member comfortable. He, in return, always took the time to say thank you.

Floyd died quietly in his own home, supported by a community of loving friends—a community of relationships. More recently, I experienced the other side of this scenario. A friend, in the final phase of cancer, found herself alone—and lonely—in a "transitional care unit" of a large, distant metropolitan hospital. She had been, in earlier years, a point person in our little village's local political issues: proactive, pivotal, and peaceful. She was a child of the sixties and had given her children the gift of freedom. That freedom helped each of them cultivate strong differentiations—too strong, as it turned out. Their busy lives rushed past her as she slowed down under the weight of her illness. She found herself looking death in the face all by herself in a cold, impersonal institution.

Penny's story isn't unusual. American cultural individualism has increasingly institutionalized more and more of the dying, as well as delegating their care to experts. While this model might offer the most technologically advanced, scientific medical treatment available, contacts with the people to whom the dying are most attached—and whose presence could offer the utmost comfort—are frequently thought to interfere with the treatment plan. Friends and family are just messy inconveniences.

This is exactly where Penny found herself—dying alone behind a closed door. She had excellent medical care but felt socially alienated. She had become despondent and had stopped eating in order to speed up her ultimate destiny. Death is denied in American hospitals. Ward curtains are drawn around the bed so that no one can see the dead body.

Fortunately, Penny's story has a different ending. Penny had been a part of our small alpine mountain community for years before moving to the large metropolitan area where she was facing the end of life. She had moved in order to get more sophisticated medical care—which she got. But she paid the price of becoming a commodity.

The large, urban hospital didn't employ a relationship-based service model and Penny felt incrementally more and more depersonalized. When members from our little rural community reached out to her and offered to bring her back here to die—among friends and familiar surroundings—she rebounded. Through the coordinated efforts of our local collectivist community, we were able to bring her back to a noninstitutionalized environment where she had a supportive network of peers.

Once she was free of the hospital, the tension and pressure began to fall away. She began to eat again and summoned the strength to transition with dignity. Her last days were free of fear. Time was incredibly valuable. All the crushing worries, torments, and pain of the preceding months dissipated.

Penny's death was like those in Kenya, where loved ones sing hymns as they bid their friends and family goodbye. The last days of life are unique for each person. They are very personal, and very private. The closeness of loved ones and familiar surroundings—no matter how simple—offers a context for shared reflection, contemplation, and completion. Given the options of institutional sterility (albeit sophisticated medical care) or community relationships (complete with the "messy inconvenience" of family and friends interrupting the treatment plan), my choice will be the latter.

The High Cost of Low Prices

In July, 1995, over 700 Chicago residents, most of them old and impoverished, died in a short but devastating heat wave. The social autopsy of this disaster highlighted an increase in the number of people living alone, including seniors who outlived or became estranged from their social networks. It also revealed the number of people using social withdrawal and reclusion as survival strategies to deal with their fear of crime. Together, these conditions created a formula for disaster that the 1995 heat wave actualized for the city of Chicago—and could well happen in any of a growing number of similar settings around the United States.

Today's electronic networks, such as email, Facebook, instant messaging, and online chat have significantly preempted door-to-door and face-to-face relationships, resulting in what University of Toronto Sociologist Barry Wellman calls "networked individualism." Technology is here to stay. So how can we use it to enhance, rather than diminish, strong interpersonal ties?

Integrating community assets to include both tangible associations between individuals as well as informal, proximity-based social clusters, built and maintained through new media, has the potential to result in what journalist Ethan Watters refers to as "urban tribes"—groups of friends who live in the same city and supplement face-to-face interaction with new media applications. Watters foresees urban tribes replacing functions formerly served by extended families, as well as giving modern youth a way to express civic mindedness through offering a "different style of giving back."

Nourishing relationship takes time. And consumer culture hasn't encouraged people to invest time in building strong relationships. There isn't any money to be made in forming interpersonal bonds, so why bother? Time is better spent making money and shopping for cheap "stuff." And from that point of view it's a short walk to the exploitation of people—especially ones that we've never met—for one's own personal gain.

I know what you're thinking: "No way, not in twenty-first-century America." Enter "cheap labor"—and the high cost of low prices. The global economy has opened the American marketplace to goods from countries that routinely allow abuse of working people. From the clothing we wear to the toys our children play with, store shelves are stocked with goods made in sweatshops where workers labor in unsafe conditions and are paid wages so low they must struggle to feed and shelter their families. This is because, from the perspective of our current economic system, poverty is a good thing. Poverty increases profit margins, so its existence is beneficial to a global economy. In fact, it is in the best interests of multinational corporations and their shareholders to prolong poverty—and its supply of cheap labor—for as long as possible. "Always low prices" really means "always low respect" for fellow human beings.

Huge multinational corporations, such as Nike, Mattel, Gap, Speedo, Banana Republic, Reebok, Adidas, and Victoria's Secret (just to name a few), have all made millions on the backs of Asian sweat labor. And the buck doesn't stop there. The Department of Defense is the world's largest purchaser of American made apparel. Approximately 20,000 men and women manufacture uniforms for the armed forces—many of them working in U.S. sweatshops.

"Conduct Unbecoming: Sweatshops and the U.S. Military Uniform Industry," a report documenting sweatshop conditions prevalent at many factories with government uniform contracts, is the result of extensive research and interviews with 88 workers at eight contractors throughout the southern United States over the past several years. The report uncovers a host of abuses. The average pay at these contractors weighed in at $6.55 an hour. Few workers surveyed were able to afford their employers' healthcare benefits, if offered. One company, Columbia Sewing, didn't even offer its employees healthcare coverage. At another, 86 percent of workers interviewed had no healthcare coverage. How can we get to *fair trade* if we don't even promote sustainable relationship-based business in our own country?

Fair trade, established in 1992, advocates the payment of a higher price to developing producers, making them stakeholders in their own livelihoods. Compare this to profit-only motives that kept seventy-two Thai immigrants working under slave-like conditions in El Monte, California. In August 1995, local and Federal law enforcement agents conducted a raid on this sweatshop and found workers locked in an apartment complex surrounded by razor wire, working for 69 cents an hour. Embarrassing.

But the buck doesn't stop there either. The lust for cheap labor, and its accompanying exploitation, isn't limited to manufacturing. It even extends into education. Richard Moser, National Field Representative for the American Association of University Professors, states "the attempt to run higher education as a business is an utter failure and a national disaster in the making." The economy's recent free fall resulted in states cutting their higher education budgets just as university costs began to rise. State subsidies were down, costs were up, and enrollment shot up to a record high as unemployed adults came back to college in droves.

Universities changed the way they operated and adopted corporate models. They started looking for places to make budget cuts. With personnel costs consuming the lion's share of their budgets, administrators found their money problems solved by hiring a type of teacher that few people have heard of: the adjunct professor. Adjuncts originally were local professionals who would teach an occasional college class on a part-time basis. The journalist, for example, would teach a course on news writing, or a retired judge would speak about jurisprudence.

Then, however, colleges saw them as something else: cheap labor. Academic sharecroppers. Most have doctorates and are willing to teach a class for as little as $1,500 per semester. Divide their net pay by hours worked per week and it comes out to something like $11.00 per hour.

In her controversial documentary, *Degrees of Shame,* Barbara Wolf calls adjuncts "the migrant workers of the information economy." Colleges across the country, primarily in urban areas, are hiring them by the hundreds. They get no health benefits, and they are only hired by the semester: they can be let go at any time. No benefits, no job security, and low pay—outsourcing and higher education have finally met.

In 1970, adjunct faculty made up 22 percent of higher education teaching staffs in the United States. By 1999, they logged 43 percent. As the economy has continued to weaken, that number has jumped to as high as 60 percent. As colleges have incrementally morphed into corporations, the trend has moved toward viewing students as consumers. It's kind of a McUniversity model. These same colleges make a lot of noise about their commitment to sustainability, including social responsibility, but their exploitation of adjuncts is quite embarrassing. In fact, this could be viewed as the creation of white-collar sweatshops.

The airlines get low marks, too, when it comes to paying professionals. Do you want the person sitting in the cockpit of your next flight to be underpaid just so that you can get cheap flights? Consider the February 2009 crash of Colgan Air flight 3407 near Buffalo, New York, which killed all forty-nine people aboard and one person on the ground. First Officer Rebecca Shaw earned $26 an hour and was guaranteed seventy-five hours of work each month, putting her salary at $23,400 a year. Here we go again: no benefits, no job security, and low pay. Sweatshops with wings.

Cheap Meat

When interviewed, documentary filmmaker Michael Moore responded to a question about whether every American was entitled to health care. His reply, applicable here, was, "We have to decide what kind of people we are." He was referring to our national character. Who are we? What kind of society do we want to become? Are we interested in creating a world that works for everyone . . . or one that only works for an elite few?

Americans' love affair with cheap stuff—including education and airfares—has been one of the biggest roadblocks standing in the way of sustainable relatedness. In the same way that consumer culture has moved toward valuing profit over people, it has put profit before nature. The U.S. agricultural industry, for example, can now produce unlimited quantities of meat and grains at remarkably cheap prices. But it does so at a high cost to the environment, animals, and humans.

Though Americans might like to imagine their food being produced the way their grandfathers did it, it's more likely that their burger came from a concentrated animal feeding operation (CAFO), where 1,000 or more head of livestock are kept in overcrowded, unventilated, infected, and infested indoor feedlots, where they are fattened up for slaughter as fast as possible. Today's factory farms are large industrial facilities, a far cry from the green pastures and red barns that most Americans imagine. The animals in these facilities are not considered animals at all; they are food-producing machines.

The problem is that animals aren't widgets with legs. They are living creatures and there are consequences to packing them in prison-like conditions.[2]

Doesn't anyone ever wonder where all of that manure goes? To survive and grow in that much sludge, factory-farmed animals need antibiotics—which then leads, inevitably, to antibiotic resistant bacteria. "These antibiotics are not given to sick animals," says Representative Louise Slaughter, who is sponsoring a bill to limit antibiotic use on CAFOs. "It's a preventative measure because they are kept in pretty unspeakable conditions."[3]

Something has gone terribly wrong with the relationship between human beings and the animals they rely upon for food. And whatever is wrong is wrong on a huge scale, as traditional animal husbandry has given way to industrialization. But Americans want cheap burgers, and Big Agriculture is good at hushing up what they do to keep the costs down. As one commentator stated in *Contemporary Issues in Animal Agriculture,* an agribusiness textbook: "One of the best things agriculture has going for it is that most people in the developed countries . . . haven't a clue how animals are raised and processed. For modern animal agriculture, the less the consumer knows, the better."

And consumers don't know. There's a lot of distance between the CAFO and their dinner table. They buy beef all neatly arranged on a styrofoam tray, shrink wrapped in plastic, from a squeaky clean refrigerator case. It's a commodity, not an animal. And they are certainly not aware that it was an animal that was badly treated—objectified—like a mere cog in the industrial wheel.

Is this the best that humans are capable of? We tried a different tactic on the farm. We raised cattle, pigs, and chickens for our own consumption—not an undertaking that we took lightly. We were keenly aware that we were killing sentient beings in order to eat. It was pretty intense. We had a farm rule that you couldn't eat meat unless you could participate in every aspect of its production. *Every* aspect—including killing it.

All of our animals were raised organically and humanely in natural habitats. We really did have the green pastures and red barns that most Americans dreamed about. Our cattle grazed on the farm's rolling hillsides. They shared their pastures with the horses who they eyed with great curiosity. They were especially fascinated when the children came out and wiggled up onto the horses' backs to take long, slow rides around the fields and over the brooks.

The hogs lived outdoors in a hardwood grove and ate organic grains and vegetables culled from our gardens. Each year, we prepared carefully for the arrival of the baby piglets by building inviting safe-spaces for them to scramble into to get out of the way—and avoid getting crushed—as the mother pigs flopped their massive bodies down in the shade of a big maple to nurse them.

The chickens roamed free-range, feasting on organic corn and dusting themselves every afternoon in the rich, dry soil out behind the barn. They ferreted out bugs and pecked at grasses from dawn to dusk, at which time they roosted all over the paddock fences. We raised all of our animals carefully and offered them the best life that we knew how to give them.

When the day came to butcher any one of them, we did it ourselves, just the way our grandparents had—no surrogates, no middle men. We thanked each animal for the sacrifice that they were making. It was humbling. So humbling, in fact, that, over time, it became impossible for me to continue to eat meat. It got harder and harder to refer to what had been a sleek, shiny pig as a pork chop.

The day came when I couldn't pull the trigger. I realized that I wasn't honoring my relationship with these animals. I was objectifying them. Watching a steer who had loafed happily in the pastures all summer become a lifeless carcass—within a matter of just a few hours—took away any illusions that I still had left about meat eating.

I would have been denying my own freedom, behaving like an inert object, to continue. I could hear Sartre admonishing that I was guilty of bad faith if I didn't take responsibility for my own choices. I knew I had to make some changes.

A Dozen Things You Can Do

- Study the myths to begin learning about the archetypal dimensions of interpersonal relationship. Robert A. Johnson's trilogy, *He*, *She*, and *We* are excellent resources to kick off this exploration.
- Prepare an advance health care directive (that is, a living will), in accordance with your state laws, and appoint a power of attorney. File these papers in multiple locations so that they are easily accessible in the event of an unforeseen medical emergency.
- Make it a personal policy to not patronize any commercial enterprises that profit from sweat labor. Likewise, boycott commercial brands that are manufactured in third world sweatshops.
- Take some time and try to determine how, ideally, you would like to die. Do you prefer to die at home or in a care facility? Are there any particular rituals or traditions that you would like observed as you draw close to death? Give this issue some very serious thought. Once you have a clear idea of the things that are the most important to you, write them up in a formal statement. Give this document to the person who will be responsible for overseeing your final days and hours.
- Sponsor neighborhood crafting events as a way to develop collectivism. The crafted items can later be sold at area fairs, facilitating yet another layer of collective community.
- Read *The Tibetan Book of the Dead*, whose actual title is *The Great Liberation upon Hearing in the Intermediate State* or *Bardo Thodol*. This book offers a compelling perspective on the spiritual significance of death.
- Volunteer at your local hospice. Get familiar with the myriad of options available to dying persons in your area.
- Buy fair trade products. Make this a firm ethical commitment.
- Experiment with vegetarianism. Get a vegetarian cookbook and sample some of the recipes. Once you begin to identify some favorites, begin to have regular "vegetarian nights" for your family dinners.

- Use technology to extend your circle of friendships by using electronic networking to create "urban tribes." You could, for example, host a potluck picnic and, instead of sending out personal invitations, post the event to your Facebook friends—allowing them to post it to their friends and so on. You'll be surprised at who shows up, and your circle of friends will grow.
- Advocate for benefit packages for part-time employees.
- Visit a CAFO. Observe the production practices and policies. Decide whether or not you can continue to purchase meat that was produced under these conditions.

12

Later Experiments in Freedom

When you are inspired by some great purpose, some extraordinary project, all your thoughts break their bonds: Your mind transcends limitations, your consciousness expands in every direction, and you find yourself in a new, great, and wonderful world.

—Patanjali

I thought that becoming a vegetarian would be simple. It would be an easy, singular change—I would just stop eating meat, right? Wrong. I had no idea how many other facets of my life were going to be affected by this decision. And then there was the way that the change retooled my perception. It wasn't just a dietary change: it was the first step in what turned out to be a whole lifestyle change.

Consciousness is nebulous. It plays hide and seek with us—darting around the edges of our perceptual field until we are ready to inhabit new ways of being. Then, like a tiger pouncing on a mouse, it takes us into its paw and shakes us until, through the intensity of the moment, we find ourselves morphing into a new person. So I stopped eating meat. And some other things happened as well. The tiger put me back down on different ground—literally.

The Experiments Move to California

If I connect the dots, I can see that my move to California started with the decision to become a vegetarian. It wasn't a straight shot—much more circuitous—but becoming a vegetarian triggered a chain of events that facilitated my move from Vermont to California.

One of the reasons that I ate meat in Vermont was to stay warm. Vermont is cold—seriously cold. I worked outdoors with the horses, in temperatures where I was burning tons of calories per hour and needed fats to deliver a lot of calories in a small download. My winter wardrobe already resembled the Pillsbury Doughboy, so I couldn't just put on more layers. Eating beef and pork had always kept the heat turned up, and once I eliminated them from my diet, I felt cold.

Since Vermont was not yet wired, I logged some hours in the stacks of the local library reading about the warming effects of avocados, olives, dates, persimmons, and apricots. I also learned that potassium-rich foods, like macadamia nuts and sunflower seeds, stoked the internal furnace. Sulfur-residue foods, including broccoli, garlic, and onion got good marks for regulating the thermometer, too. There was only one problem. Most of these foods grew in California and we were radical locavores.

Since I couldn't grow these foods in Vermont, I decided to move where they were. This decision sounds, in the telling, as if it was much easier than it actually was. Compounding my decision to move where I could more realistically accommodate my new diet was a divorce from my husband of twenty-two years as well as my two children going off to college. I also had a lot of trepidation about leaving Vermont. The Green Mountain State had been a mother to me: nurturing and maturing me into a more hardy version of myself. I found myself wondering if I could fall in love with somewhere else the way that I had fallen in love with Vermont. It was definitely a time of change for me. It marked a definite transition—and a very important one. I needed to think deeply about where I could live a sustainable lifestyle, create a sense of place and honor core psychological values that had awakened in me over the past two decades.

I knew that my new home had to have healthful air, water, and soil. It also had to have four distinct seasons. Living twenty-two years in Vermont had given me an appreciation for the unique gifts of each season, and I didn't want to lose any of them: I coveted sun and snow, foliage and spring rains. I knew that I was looking for a space that would accommodate my home and barn, food production, recreation, and dressage activities, as well as invite fellow travelers.

I wanted to be located amidst natural beauty, so that my space would provide mental and psychological well-being, as well as stimulate and nurture my spiritual explorations. And, of course, I had my heart set on mountains. Big mountains. I was looking for a place that would inspire me to become more than I was.

Not Just California—But Mount Shasta!

Mount Shasta is a big mountain, 14,179 feet, to be exact. The village sits at the foot of the mountain. It is a rural community. The income base is broad, not dependent on a single industry. The three strongest sources of income are transfer payments (such as retirement monies), service industries, and tourism. Nonetheless, the local economy, in 2010, is plagued by an 18.10 percent unemployment rate. More important, though, than economic conditions are its stable *social* conditions—its close-knit and nurturing community.

People in Mount Shasta often joke about the area being a happenstance intentional community. Most are ecologically sensitive and were attracted to Mount Shasta's exceptional air quality and clean, pure water. It appealed to me, too.

Water is the new oil. Even though 70 percent of Earth is covered with water, only 3 percent is fit for human consumption, of which two-thirds is frozen in largely uninhabited ice caps and glaciers, leaving 1 percent available for consumption. According to the United Nations, 50 percent of all hospital beds worldwide are occupied by patients who are ill from contaminated water. So clean, pure water was a big draw. Water quality in Mount Shasta, California is sixty on an EPA scale of one hundred (higher is better).

When I moved to Mount Shasta, one of my first tasks was to drill two wells on my new property. I dowsed the property and chose my spots carefully. One well is fifty-five feet deep and pumps sixty gallons a minute and the other is sixty-seven feet deep, pumping one-hundred gallons a minute. The water from both wells is crystal clear, clean, and potable. I struck "oil."

Mount Shasta has an average of 229 sunny days per year, with summer highs around eighty-five degrees. All of that water, in conjunction with sunshine and warm temperatures, assured that I could develop high yield organic vegetable gardens. This was a nice step up from the average of 157 sunny days, and summer highs of eighty degrees, in Central Vermont. I began to think solar in earnest. And, I'm still thinking about it. That's not to say that I am weighing the pros and cons. We've all done that and know that the plusses outweigh the minuses. That's old news.

What prevents people from going solar are the costs. It is an expensive transition. And that's just what I've been thinking about—putting money that I might otherwise have put into investment products into my solar transition. The idea of investing in my own sustainable lifestyle, instead of in an unpredictable and highly manipulated "market," makes any old, lingering resistance about the expense of the transition irrelevant. My "portfolio" these days is *highly* diversified—full of solar panels, greenhouses, composting systems, and alternative transportation.

Slow Money

It's my own variation on slow money: building a personal economy that is postindustrial finance and postindustrial agriculture. The concept of slow money is dedicated to slow, small, and local. It's about designing capital markets built around preservation and restoration instead of extraction and consumption, offering ways to invest for the future that are grounded in local, community-based, mission-positive enterprise.

The principles of the slow money movement include bringing money back down to earth—literally. This movement sees investment as more than venture capital. It's nurture capital, built around principles of carrying capacity, care of the commons, sense of place, and nonviolence.

Slow money proponents see the economic crisis, paired with increasingly alarming news about the effects of climate change and environmental degradation, as an opportunity for a new economic paradigm. Woody Tasch, spokesperson for the movement and author of *Inquiries into the Nature of Slow Money,* says that people think of self-organizing microfinance as a shift in consumer dollars rather than as investments, whereas it is really a kind of investment. He urges Americans to rethink funding traditional investment instruments that support exploitive and extractive industries and to, instead, consider slow money methods that might take longer to get a return on investment dollars—and the returns might be lower—but the investor knows that she has made the earth a better place to live.

Instead of thinking about "making a killing," according to Tasch, we should think in terms of making a living.

Building the Hermitage

California real estate prices made me do another thing that Americans aren't all that good at—and that's to quit thinking so big. Think smaller. I decided to buy only as much land as I needed and could care for. I implemented intensive techniques for all of the systems involved in my operation—from gardening and horse husbandry to woodlot management.

I found that intensive planning reduced wasted space to a minimum, concentrated work efforts to create an ideal environment, and yielded better results with less labor. I was used to seeing spacious, green rolling pastures dotted with horses. Each horse, however, only requires an acre of well-managed land for forage, movement, and relaxation. The key is management: sturdy, safe fences; daily cleaning to reduce parasite infestation; and a combination of sun and shade. I built my three-rail fences out of recycled lumber, protected them with biodegradable, organic plant-based, and zero VOC terra-cotta paints that, aesthetically, blend in with my wooded hillside.

My multiphase composting system returns composted manure to

the base of the trees each autumn, delivering warm organic nutrients to their root systems all winter. My hefty wells irrigate the paddocks for a few minutes each summer evening, keeping them dust free and cool, converting this alpine desert into a high-altitude rain forest. And the ecosystem has responded in like kind. All kinds of wild edibles have sprung up, while the incidence of pesky insects has been almost eliminated.

Butterflies and birds flutter above the paddocks, and wild roses and grapes stand like sentinels against the fence posts. I trim any low hanging branches from the trees and they are cut and cured for next season's kindling.

When it came time to plan my horse barn, I had an encounter with my own unconscious. I went on autopilot and started sketching out plans for a large center aisle stall barn like the one I had built in Vermont—until the light bulb finally went off in my head. Who do those big center aisles really serve? Do the horses need them—or even like them? The more I thought about it, the more I realized that the center aisle was really just a place to store "stuff": extra buckets, brushes, blankets, boots, and feed tubs. Moreover, did the horses even like being locked into indoor stalls?

This was California, and even the most severe winter weather was no match for Vermont. Why not build a system more appropriate to my new setting where the horses could choose to be inside or outside on their own? I got excited about my new vision and enthusiastically set about building a series of individual horse houses at various places in their paddocks. I made them large and airy, with heavy joists to accommodate Mount Shasta's snow loads.

Each one is heavily insulated with recycled denim. The denim is 100 percent recycled, organic, and—since it's good old-fashioned cotton—it didn't off-gas any nasty chemicals. It installed quickly and easily, and didn't require any special equipment or protective clothing. The insulation keeps the horses cool in the summer and, more important, tight and snug in the winter. Since Northern California is no stranger to wildfires, I had to keep fire retardation in mind. I used large wooden timbers instead of dimension lumber, site-built trusses rather than using manufactured ones, and chose metal roofing—which is also great for encouraging snow to slide off.

Gardening at the Hermitage

I carried my intensive land-use blueprint into planning my vegetable gardens, too, finding all kinds of ways to grow more food on less land. I experimented with combinations of raised beds, wide rows, vertical trellising, intercropping, and succession planting.

Traditionally gardens consist of long, single rows, spaced three feet apart. Much of the garden area consists of the space between rows. The idea of traditional, single-row planting started with the use of mules to cultivate the garden. Out of habit, many gardeners still use this system. An intensive garden, on the other hand, keeps space—as well as water and labor—to a minimum. And, anyway, who still has mules?

I fell in love with my intensive gardens and found myself snapping digital pictures of them constantly. They were beautiful—and they grew so much food! My unframed raised beds, arranged just wide enough to reach across, are ideal for growing vegetables and herbs. A higher percentage of my available growing space is used, there is less room for weeds to grow, and water is used more efficiently. The yield per square foot from raised beds is as much as twice the yield from conventional single row gardening.

My vertical trellising—done right off of the raised beds—gives the gardens "height" and are part of what make them so artistic. I attach old bale hay twine to the top of recovered tree branches that I position, like poles, in the soil. The twine comes down to the ground, where I secure each strand with a rock, ending up with little "tipis" for peas, beans, cucumbers, and squash to crawl up. These plants take up much less ground space and, though the yield per plant may be less, the yield per square foot is much greater.

My garden is surrounded with manzanita bushes on the back side—nature's trellises. I plant my pumpkins and winter squash on this side and let them meander out of the garden and over onto the bushes. By late summer, little pumpkins and buttercup squash can be seen peeking out from the leaves of the bushes—hanging there like giant ornaments! Hermitage guests with an artistic flair enjoy photographing the adorned manzanita—a collage of bush and bulb.

Interplanting—growing two or more types of vegetables in the same place at the same time—is visually pleasing as well as functional. I plant long-season, slow-maturing peppers right beside short-season, quick maturing radishes. I harvest the radishes before they begin to be crowded by the peppers. The little red radish tops sticking up through the soil add a potpourri of color to the pepper plants' verdant green foliage. I also plant smaller plants close to larger plants—radishes at the base of broccoli, for example—and combine shade tolerant species like lettuce, spinach, and celery in the shadow of the taller, trellised crops. Since most garden pests are usually crop-specific, interplanting also helps keep insect and disease problems under control.

When one type of vegetable is harvested, I plant something new in its place. Succession planting really maximizes an intensive garden. Once the heavy harvest of the season is complete, I replant cool-season crops—broccoli, lettuce, kale, collards, peas—to go into the fall and early winter. I harvest kale and chard from under light, early winter, dustings of snow. They are sweeter in the cold weather and it makes me feel like the gardening season hasn't ended. And, in many ways, it hasn't.

The cold frames protect winter greens and tomatoes ripen in the greenhouse until Thanksgiving. After the days shorten and temperatures drop, I move my gardening efforts indoors. The kitchen comes to life as I set up sprouting stations, wheatgrass trays, and culinary herbs on the windowsill.

The fall kitchen, with woodstove ablaze, becomes the hub of the Hermitage. Baskets of harvested vegetables and wildcrafted fruits are put by. Large bunches of dried, wildcrafted herbs and teas, hanging from the ceiling beams, are carefully crushed and prepared for winter use. Mountain sage, gathered from the side of Mount Shasta, is skillfully rolled into aromatic smudge sticks, which are piled by the woodstoves.

Going Raw

Since fresh produce is available year-round in California, I became interested in plant-based raw food diets. I decided to try it out about six years ago—and have been "raw" ever since! My initial impression that a raw foods diet was going to be spartan—carrot and celery sticks—couldn't have been further from the truth. Meals—complete with extraordinary desserts—at the Hermitage are gourmet. And the health benefits have been extraordinary: increased energy, glowing skin, and weight loss.

Our raw food diet is based on unprocessed and uncooked plant foods, such as fresh fruit and vegetables, sprouts, seeds, grains, beans, nuts, and dried fruits. The raw food diet contains no trans-fat and fewer saturated fats than the standard American diet. It is also low in sodium and high in potassium, magnesium, folate, fiber, and health-promoting plant chemicals called phytochemicals. And raw plant foods are extremely enzyme rich: enzymes are a vital element in maintaining good health.

Enzymes are responsible for every reaction in the human body. Without enzymes, we simply die. Enzymes dissolve the clots responsible for strokes and heart attacks. The raw food diet reduces the risk of cardiovascular disease, as well as diabetes and cancer. So, my progression had gone from vegetarianism to *raw* vegetarianism. What next? You guessed it: raw veganism.

Veganism

I had already converted from pasteurized dairy products to raw ones, but on the way to veganism I considered giving them up completely. That is, until I discovered raw, vegan milks, cheeses and yogurts.

The human body is not designed to digest cow milk and related dairy products: the idea of milk being healthy is largely an advertising ploy. As many as 75 percent of people in the world may be lactose intolerant and many people suffer from undiagnosed milk allergies or sensitivities. The American Dietetic Association reports that breast cancer is most prevalent in countries where women consume high-fat, animal-based diets.

In Asia, where milk consumption is rare, breast cancer is almost unheard of. Japanese women who follow a more Western-style, meat- and dairy-based diet are eight times more likely to develop breast cancer than their counterparts who eat a plant-based diet not containing dairy products. Internationally renowned nutrition expert Dr. T. Colin Campbell points to China, a traditionally non-milk-drinking country, where cancer deaths among women aged thirty-five to sixty-four averaged less than 9 per 100,000, as opposed to 44 per 100,000 in the United States.

Even if the health benefits hadn't swayed me (which, though, they did), the cuisine sealed the deal. After a bit of trial and error, I learned to make outstanding raw, artisan vegan cheeses and yogurts. Raw coconut yogurt is about as good as it gets: thick, sweet, and creamy. And, by making it myself, I am assured that the acidophilus cultures are fresh and plentiful. And, if that's not enough, there is the added bonus of not requiring any plastic packaging. Win-win.

In the same way that the yogurt sweetens the start of my day, the nut cheeses light up my evenings. Sitting down by the woodfire, book in hand, with a little round of tarragon-rosemary crusted cashew cheese and a pile of dehydrated, raw crackers is my own little corner of heaven. I usually sip a glass of my homemade kombucha tea with it.

When fermented, kombucha creates a sparkling beverage, similar to champagne in taste. Friends of the drink claim that it improves vitality, raises T cell numbers, lowers blood pressure, eases aches and pains of arthritis, helps resist eczema and digestive disorders, and reduces risk of cancer. Some research even suggests that kombucha has antimicrobial effects against harmful bacteria like E. coli and, possibly, anti-fungal properties. The first documented use of kombucha was in 221 B.C.E. in China, during the Tsin Dynasty, when it was called "The Tea of Immortality."

Finding My Tribe

But being healthy wouldn't be of so much value if it were a solitary experience. Fortunately, it hasn't been. I found my tribe in Mount Shasta. The current community is a seed that has been growing since the 1987 Harmonic Convergence.

Mount Shasta is a laboratory for the future, interweaving sociality, spirituality, and environmentalism. In the shadow of the big mountain, ancient traditions and advanced technologies walk hand-in-hand. And people's eyes are on the horizon—on tomorrow and tomorrow and tomorrow.

Being a part of this type of community has stretched me. My children, now grown, reflect my process back to me. Old, stuck parts of me have been shed—often as a product of a lot of rigorous depth work. New, experimental parts of me have emerged.

Mount Shasta is a community of people who walk softly and try to leave no trace. When I planted a plum tree last week, nobody here asked me why I would bother since, in all probability, it won't bear fruit in my lifetime. People here got it. I planted it for the Good Life—of tomorrow, and tomorrow, and tomorrow.

A Dozen Things You Can Do

- Experiment with not eating any meat for a week. What was this experience like for you? Did you notice any changes in your body or mind?
- Use a stainless steel, ecofriendly, BPA-free Klean Kanteen for carrying drinking water, instead of using commercially bottled water.
- Learn about intensive gardening techniques and decide which methods might work for your particular space. Plan to use the ones that will allow you to grow "the most food on the least land."
- Get an estimate on a solar hot water system.
- Create a natural environment for your animals. Try to reduce artificial domestication of your pets and restore, as much as possible, natural habitats.
- Place the point of a compass on your town and draw a 100-mile radius around it. Experiment with only eating foods that are produced within this radius.
- Make a recipe for raw flaxseed crackers. Instead of baking, sun dry them on cookie sheets.
- After you have harvested your summer garden produce, replant a fall garden. Select vegetables that thrive in cool weather, such as broccoli, kale, and other hardy greens.
- Learn to make green smoothies in your blender. Incorporate them into your weekly meal plans.
- Sun dry slices of zucchini and tomatoes, fresh from your garden (or the farmer's market). After they are dry, put them in reused plastic bags to carry with you, for healthy snacking, when you are away from home.
- Make your own fruit leather. Puree fall fruits and pour the batter onto cookie sheets. Dry in the sun. Flip over from time to time until the batter has become a sticky leather. Roll-up and store.
- Plant a tree for the next generation.

13

Back to the Garden

Two paths meet here; no one has yet followed either to its end. This long lane stretches back for an eternity. And the long lane out there, that is another eternity. They contradict each other, these paths; they offend each other face to face; and it is here at this gateway that they come together.

—Friedrich Wilhelm Nietzsche

The Woodstock Festival, held on Max Yasgur's six-hundred-acre dairy farm in the rural town of Bethel, New York, in August of 1969, was an early chapter in the new story being written for American culture. It was a three-day "temporary commune," where time stood still. A modern-day Canterbury Tale, it heralded the pilgrimage back to the land. It was the year of the Beatles swansong, the first manned moon landing, the hippie protests over U.S. involvement in Vietnam, Chappaquiddick, the Manson murders, the Stonewall riots—and Woodstock.

Yasgur's farm reflected the back-to-the-land spirit of the counter-culture and was undoubtedly a catalyst in my eventual move, a few years later, to Vermont. Countercultural icons Crosby, Stills, Nash & Young gave voice to the spirit of the movement when they sang about us being "billion year old carbon" that has to get itself "back to the garden."

The Making of a Counterculture

By the time *I* got to Woodstock, it was already "a half a million strong." I will never forget the adrenaline rush I felt when I looked down into that muddy field and saw all of those people. The air was pregnant with emotion—alive with soul. I remember thinking that the fruit of the 1960s social revolution had ripened—that I was seeing the capstone of an era devoted to human development. The cynics retorted, of course, that it was a fitting, ridiculous end to an era of naiveté. Maybe, in retrospect, it was a little bit of both. But either way, there were a half a million people, all gathered in one place, who wanted to create a new paradigm, a new world—a world that worked just a little bit better for everyone. It was a moment in history when a portal of opportunity opened.

The movement was labeled "*counter*-cultural" by Theodore Roszak's[1] *The Making of a Counter Culture,* which probably, inadvertently, was one of the shots in its foot. Sure, there were those of us who put our hands to the till, but for every one of us that did, there were hundreds of others who got so caught up in the culturally legislated, exterior demands of career, parenthood, marriage, home ownership, and divorce, that they forgot all about the door that opened at Woodstock. They traded the counterculture for mass culture—the established order.

But forty years later, these same baby boomers are looking back as they plan for retirements that, for most, are now delayed years beyond their expectations. The current economic downturn has brought them full circle. It is another moment in history when a portal of opportunity is open. But, this time, it's not quite the same—and that difference just might be enough to change the world! This time, a recycled version of those '60s countercultural ideals are gaining credence as potentially critical *mass cultural* issues.

For one thing, it's not just the young people this time around. It's intergenerational. The young people are worried about the world that they have inherited, and the boomers, if for no other reason than the radical devaluation of their 401(k)s, are starting to wonder why they ever left the garden in the first place. Furthermore, someone would be hard pressed to call this an era of naiveté. This is harsh, stark reality. The problems we face are real and they affect the whole world.

Roszak had questioned whether or not the counterculture would be able to overturn the established order. He defined the established order as a rationalized, relentless quest for efficiency and order. It was maintained by its reliance upon exteriority, as opposed to any serious consideration of interior states. In this structure, spin doctors and public relations firms assumed greater and greater prominence.

Roszak cheered on a counterculture that was intent upon overthrowing scientific materialism, with its entrenched commitment to an egocentric mode of consciousness. Pointing to the clock as the archetypal machine of modernity, he was concerned about how humans had adapted themselves to machines, rather than vice-versa. Bemoaning runaway manufacturing and industrialization, he wrote, "Commercial vulgarism is one of the endemic pests of twentieth-century Western life, like flies that swarm to sweets in the summer."[2]

Now, forty years later, as one system after another—from economic to environmental—is collapsing under the weight of nonsustainability, the counterculture is well poised to not only overturn, but to replace, the established order. Those adding voice to the movement are reaching a critical mass and are close to being the proverbial "half a million strong."

According to Dr. Paul H. Ray and Sherry Ruth Anderson, in *The Cultural Creatives: How 50 Million People Are Changing the World*, there are 50 million people, 26 percent of the population, who they call "cultural creatives," hidden within America. Ray and Anderson note that these people have a well-developed social consciousness and a guarded optimism for the future. They are disenchanted with owning more stuff, with status display, and with the glaring social inequities of race. They are critical of almost every big institution of modern society, including corporations and government.

This cultural group, drawn from all classes, races, education, income levels, and social backgrounds, has emerged only during the past 50 years and, according to the Ray and Anderson, now forms a coherent subculture. Ray and Anderson argue that cultural creatives hold the potential for radically reshaping the values and material realities, the deep structure, of American life. The counterculture is finding its way into mainstream culture's slow walk toward postconsumerism. A lot has happened in forty years. This is the time that we have been waiting for—and we are the people that we have been waiting for. We really *are* billion-year-old carbon—and it really *is* time to get back to the garden.

Back to the Garden

First of all, we need to be clear that the itinerary "back to the garden" has two, intimately intertwined destinations. The first one is obvious. It's immanence. It's getting dirt under our fingernails and tending to our individual human gardens—planting, harvesting, recycling, bicycling, slowing down, conscious eating, composting, interpersonal caring, and creating community. It's getting our acts together about how we treat the earth, ourselves, and each other.

If we can pull this off, we will begin to see the second destination just over the horizon. It's transcendence. The way down is the way up. The more we sink our roots into the Earth and assure a sustainable future for all of humankind, the more we reach our branches up into the Garden, the mythic state of perfection from which mankind fell.

This is an opportunity to wake up, to remember, and to reconcile soil and source—the garden and the Garden. These are living ideas and people get excited about "going back." There's a catch, though. There is no "going back." The future stretches out in front of us. The path leads *forward*. But it's not a disintegrated forwardness that goes, like a runaway horse, headlong into perilous terrain. We've already done that. If it is going to be sustainable, this time the forward impetus—the script for the New American Dream—must be charged with *reintegrating* the cast-off wisdom of our ancestors.

The script for the New American Dream requires a new meta-map, a new structural account of why, how, and where things fit together. Such a map will need certain systemic features that convincingly integrate human existence with the wider universe.

It goes without saying that the map must be socially constructed in a way that forms the foundations of different modus operandi. We can't afford to make the same mistake again, erroneously assuming that dissociated rationality is the culmination of conscious evolution. The consequences have been devastating.

Our era has been stripped of inner meaning and the external world was rendered into mere resources. The old American Dream was built on an illusion: the illusion that only half of reality mattered—the measurable, quantitative, material part. Our rejection of myth led to disenchantment of the self and the world. Now, the great task of post-consumer society is to reintegrate them. Thinking that we can simply "fix" the socioeconomic structure and put things back the way they were is naive. It's a band-aid that doesn't address sustainability.

We are like Humpty Dumpty. Things might appear to work for a while—until the next wave of anomalies—but then, soon enough, the fatal flaws of an unsustainable system will again become apparent. It is a matter of time before all the King's horses and all the King's men won't be able to put us together again.

The script for the New American Dream can't be written by spin doctors and vested corporate interests. It needs to be written from scratch, by one person at a time, who has begun to live an "examined life," and, consequently, to awaken to who one really is.

Know Thyself

Socrates encouraged his fellow citizens to live an "examined life," confirming the Delphic motto to "Know Thyself." He believed that it was only through self-knowledge, through an understanding of one's own psyche, that one could find happiness. For Socrates, happiness, or *eudaimonia,* was not the consequence of external circumstances, such as wealth, power, or reputation, but was the result of living a life that was good for the soul.

Eudaimonia is generally translated into English as "happiness," and while this is adequate, it does not entirely capture the meaning of the Greek word. One important difference is that happiness seems closely bound up with a subjective assessment of the quality of one's life, whereas *eudaimonia* refers to an objectively desirable life—a life that one has consciously chosen to live in accord with certain principles.

Socrates brought to the developing Western mind an awareness of the central significance of the soul, establishing it for the first time as the seat of the individual waking consciousness.[3] This concept of happiness, then, is soul-centered, and is not a type of superficial cheeriness.

In *Against Happiness,* scholar Eric G. Wilson offers an important correction to the contemporary idea that happiness is akin to "dying with the most toys" or winning the lottery. Wilson feels that what most people consider to be happiness is actually a living death, as its shallow exteriority is not sufficiently soul-centered. He argues that melancholia, or the dark night of the soul, is a part of *eudaimonia,* as melancholia is a vital force that inspires creativity, spurs ambition, and helps people form more intimate bonds with one another.

As the muse of great literature, painting, music, and innovation, melancholia is the force underlying original insight. When, for example, I listen to certain pieces of music, or appreciate various art forms, or look out my window on a rainy day, I experience a sweet sadness, a melancholic state that is actually very satisfying. In it, I am happy—deeply so. Bittersweet. A thriving culture, argues Wilson, must include this dark night of the soul as part of its *eudaimonia,* since cultural expectations of happiness will otherwise be bound up with purely subjective assessments of the quality of one's individual life instead of with broader commitments to human flourishing.

As our individual souls—the part of us that values and cultivates the Good Life—emerge, one by one, we will become a culture of souls; a culture that moves toward the Good Life. Socrates reminds us that in order to live a good life, one must know the nature and essence of the good. Otherwise, we will act blindly, on the basis of mere convention or indoctrination, calling things "good" whenever they conform to popular opinion.

Our *eudaimonia* has been buried under stuff. The cost of our affluence has been high and we have been left spiritually bankrupt. We have forgotten that we are souls, and have become mere end-users, cogs in the wheel of economy. It didn't happen overnight: it was a slow, incremental process. We forgot who we were. Cultural amnesia. Mass neuroses.

The journey back means trading cultural imperialism, with its consumerism, proliferation of advertising, unprecedented waste, exploitation of people and resources, increasing disparities in wealth and power, and commodification of free human exchange with meaning, purpose, deep life experience, and gratitude. As we remember who we are and reconnect with our souls, we will identify our signature strengths and deploy them in the service of something larger than our limited, conditioned visions. As we reach a critical mass of new consciousness, we can co-create a healthier world that is filled with hope.

Integral Consciousness

The New American Dream would value and protect natural environments so that nature would not recede, but rebound. There would be practical support for local community as we return to local banks, stores, and businesses. Less stressful lifestyles, slow food, sound sleep, eating well, and knowing our neighbors are ingredients for recycling our worn-out paradigm into one in which our decisions and policies would be driven more by our hopes than by our fears.

Our progress would be measurable by the return of people laughing together on front porches and playing softball in open fields instead of by an endless tally of "bottom lines." Men and women, having enough to live on, as John Stuart Mill suggested long ago, may well prefer "things of the soul" than the mere accumulation of material goods.

So, we are standing at a crossroads. Do we take the road less traveled by and create something new? Or does amnesia set in again once the crisis is over, and we go back to business as usual—forgetting that it just leads to a cycle of nonsustainability?

Jean Gebser, author of *The Ever-Present Origin,* constructed a psychohistorical schema of human consciousness that offers an optimistic outcome. Gebser feels that we are on the threshold of a new structure of consciousness, which he calls *the Integral.*

For Gebser, this structure integrates those which have come before and enables the human mind to transcend the limitations of three-dimensionality. This structure is difficult to describe since it depends to a great deal on experiences, not just that we have them, but on how intense they are and what we glean from them for now and for the future.

Intensity is a key characteristic of the Integral mode of consciousness. By intensity he does not mean simply an emotional relationship to experience, or the feeling or deepening of emotion itself. In order to understand Gebser's application of the term intensity, we can look at the analogy of love. Love is the driving force behind true spirituality and spiritual growth. It is quite easy to love those who are like us. This love is a three-dimensional love at best. We love those, and those things, that fit neatly into our perspectives of being and life. We choose who they are and when and how often we will extend that love to them. An integral love, a fourth-dimensional love, though, would go beyond that.

Gebser provides a powerful argument for the necessity of the emergence of integral consciousness for the welfare of humanity. He emphasized that we must *all* take responsibility, pointing to Meister Eckhart, the fifteenth-century Rhineland mystic, as an example of one who represented integral consciousness, and make a self-commitment to allow the integral consciousness to awaken—and manifest—in ourselves. In Gebser's own words:

> We have, then, an indicator as to whether or not a given person has attained this awareness or not: someone who has learned to avoid placing blame or fault on others, on the world itself, on circumstances, or "chance" in times of adversity, dissension, conflict and misfortune and seeks first in himself the reason in its fullest extent—this person should be able to see through the world in its entirety

and all its structures. Otherwise, he will be coerced or violated by either his emotions or his will, and in turn will attempt to coerce or violate the world as an act of compensation or revenge. The adage that "how we shout into the woods is how the echo will sound" is undoubtedly accurate—and the woods are the world. *Everything that happens to us, then, is only the answer and echo of what and how we ourselves are.*[4]

So it's really up to each and every one of us. It is fair to say that we must become renewed human beings—ones that shift toward values of interdependence, caring, conservation, community, and a deeper realization of our connectedness with the Earth. This shift will be evident in the how we relate, simultaneously, to both the physical and nonphysical world. Souls, not merely roles, are going to play the leading parts in the grand drama that lies ahead. We are going back to the future and, if we can stay true to our inner compass, we just might live a very, very Good Life.

A Dozen Things You Can Do

- Reflect deeply on how the economic crisis can actually cause you and your family to adopt greener, more sustainable lifestyle choices. Would you have made these changes without the catalyst of the recession? Try seeing the economic downturn as an opportunity for creating something new and better.
- Identify your own "cultural creativity." List ways in which you can reshape the values and deep structure of your life.
- Sponsor a local public dialogue about the interplay between time and money. Can you free up more time by sharing resources, bartering, and/or trading services among yourselves?
- Decide how you can reconcile "soil and source"—that is, the profane and the divine. Where are the points of conjuncture, in your life, between "heaven and earth"?
- Reintegrate the cast-off wisdom of your elders. Recall the teachings of your grandparents. Determine how you can apply various of these teachings in your current life situation.
- Support your local economy. Use local banks, shops, and professional services. Keep your dollars in your own town.
- Sponsor a monthly "neighbor's night" where all of your neighbors come together for a potluck dinner. Get to know one another.
- Visit a homeless shelter and practice an integral, fourth-dimensional love for those who do not fit into your perspectives of being and life.
- Make a habit of reading the daily news. Don't rely on just one news source. Consult multiple online sources and compare perspectives.
- Try freecycling. It's all about reuse and keeping good stuff out of landfills.
- Determine what America's "new frugality" will mean to you. Where will you make budget cuts? How will you implement

thrift? Identify areas in which you are currently unwilling or unable to cut expenses.

- Do a trash audit. This is an interesting way to learn about your lifestyle habits. Make a list of how many things you identified in your household trash that could have been recycled.

Epilogue

Do the best that you can in the place where you are, and be kind.

—Scott Nearing

I recognize that my chosen path has been somewhat extreme. I have no illusions about how far I have deviated from "the norm." That, actually, has been the whole point. But I also realize that not everyone wants to go this far out on the ledge. For some, it would be uncomfortable, foreign, or simply distasteful. The key lies in knowing that this is a *choice*—that I voluntarily chose a particular lifestyle.

My lifestyle isn't something that just happened. I made choices, in those years on the farm, that involved a desire to live in daily awareness of the consequences of each act, sought to minimize my impact on the earth through living closer to the source of life, and to reduce the processes that separated me from that source, while still maintaining a strong and vital professional orientation. It wasn't an either/or decision; it was synergistic. It was a synthesis of my roles with my soul.

We all share one Earth and, at some level, we all want to live Good Lives. So the important thing is that we each write our own story.

At what level can you engage with Sartre's condemnation to be free and still be comfortable?

Perhaps you could plant a small garden or set up some barter arrangements between yourself and friends. Maybe you could start to reduce your waste by initiating a kitchen composting system. Or your engagement could be as simple as using less plastic. You might even decide to just get your feet wet by participating in an online discussion forum about sustainability issues.

The challenge is to assess your lifestyle options and find places where you can plug in more sustainable practices, thus creating a better life for yourself and for those around you. Our lives are a composite of the choices we make. For our choices and actions to be sustainable, they must be elastic, adaptable, and creative.

People in all sorts of living environments are beginning to embrace the possibilities for creating simpler, more meaningful lives. Consider, for example, projects like the Columbia University Food Sustainability Project where vegetables are grown in an urban setting through creative, intensive methods. Or the Community Urban Sustainability Project, in Kingston, Ontario, that is working on a petition to change a city ordinance for allowing chickens to be raised within city limits. The City of Cincinnati is offering an urban gardening pilot program to transition vacant, city-owned parcels of land into food production areas.

And for the past five years, the Birmingham Urban Gardening Society (BUGS) Community and School Garden Project has helped establish schoolyard gardens in low-income districts in Alabama. The East New York Farms (ENYF) project, in Brooklyn, restores vacant land for biointensive vegetable and small-scale livestock production for sale in local farmers markets. And all over the country, private individuals are experimenting with square foot and container gardening, while others are trying out vertical growing and hydroponics.

People in Brevard County, Florida, are freecycling—giving their unwanted "stuff"away to those who do want it. Brevard's freecycle networks allow people to "shop" for free items among themselves. The Allegheny Trail Alliance, in another type of effort, is building a 152-mile bicycle and walking trail connecting Cumberland, Maryland with Pittsburgh, Pennsylvania. And, the New York State Department of Environmental Conservation is teaching schools, parents, and students how to implement waste-free lunch programs to address the sixty-seven pounds of garbage generated by the average child's disposable lunch each school year.

Ecovillages and cohousing projects like Prescott, Arizona's Manzanita Village—whose mission is to form an intentionally created community committed to fostering individual growth, group harmony, neighborliness, and the celebration of one another as individuals and as a community—are also gaining in popularity. And interest has piqued in edible landscapes, such as the one distinguishing the Vermont State House lawn as the first statehouse food garden organized by members of the public for the benefit of the public.

A more sustainable society won't come about through eco-getaways or commercially savvy environmentally friendly products. It will come through reducing consumption: voluntary simplicity. The era of single-occupant, six thousand-pound vehicles is over. So is the expectation of limitless fresh water, productive farmland, and the energy to bring food and goods to market, if we continue to apply yesterday's solutions to today's problems.

Atlanta officials met recently to discuss a previously unthinkable crisis: the city is approximately one hundred-twenty days from exhausting its supply of fresh water. And water isn't the only thing in short supply: so is petroleum, the energy that currently powers virtually every aspect of industrial society. In the time that it has taken you to read this book, 430 acres of old-growth forest will have disappeared forever. The calculus of sustainable living is becoming increasingly complex.

There is good news, though. People are beginning to get it. In just the past several years, the sustainability issue has gone from being countercultural to front-page news. But it still comes down to individual action—to you and me, each doing what we can to reduce the amount of "stuff" necessary to run our lives.

Today's problems cannot be solved with yesterday's mindset. Incremental changes are inadequate; a bold and broad agenda for systemic changes in values, lifestyles, institutions, and politics is required. But big changes happen a step at a time.

We are all walking at different paces in our individual journeys toward greener, more meaningful lives. Some of us have been on the road a while; others have just begun. That doesn't matter. What matters is that the spark is lit.

The Great Recession has been a catalyst for Americans to take inventory of their lives. And that inventory has resulted in an increasing number of people deciding to reclaim their lives—to work toward healthier families, a cleaner planet, and greater financial independence. In many ways, the economic downturn has offered an opportunity to take stock of our values and priorities.

For many people, consumer culture has lost its appeal. So have debt accumulation, time poverty, exteriority, and social alienation. Cultivating a sustainable postconsumer society will be contingent upon our ability to make a shift in consciousness. The tension between our conditioning and our consciousness is obvious. We simply can't do business as usual anymore. We need to take a long, hard look at our love affair with "stuff."

What are the broader implications of our lust for goods? If Americans can begin to burrow out from beneath the heavy burden of "stuff," the New American Dream might begin to take shape. Building social capital, creating green schools and workplaces, becoming community stakeholders, developing responsible purchasing habits, and becoming carbon shredders and upcyclers might become mainstream cultural practices.

Let's not forget that much of the robust consumer growth of the past few decades was underpinned not by income growth but by the expansion of debt and unsustainable increases in family labor hours—both of which seriously eroded the Good Life.

Americans don't need more cell phones, designer handbags, or fishing gear. We need, instead, to get serious about climate stabilization, low-carbon local economies, and healthier lifestyles. In standard economic terms, what this means is that we need to ramp up conservation, instead of consumption.

To a large degree global growth is going to depend upon American thrift. If we can relax our grip on goods—our lusty affair with stuff—and begin to live simpler, more meaningful lives, the whole world will reap the benefits. This is a huge win-win opportunity. And all we have to do to get the ball rolling is begin to live the Good Life.

Acknowledgments

Without even worrying about sounding vain, I am going to say—right upfront—that I love this book. I have loved it from its inception, but I loved it much more after the following people, to whom I am deeply indebted, generously poured hours of editorial effort. Professors Daniel A. Kealey and Heidi English tackled the rigorous job of copyediting and made it look like child's play. They corrected thousands of errant commas, missing hyphens, and random dangling participles in a draft that I naively thought was in good shape. Thank you Heidi and Kealey, for making me look literate.

Dr. Sally Cooper and Dr. Molly Brown were literary cheerleaders. They encouraged me to keep running toward the goal, even when I wasn't quite sure where it was. These two women's suggestions made the book eminently more readable. They tactfully persuaded me to turn some of my otherwise rants and ramblings into organized narratives and arguments. Thank you Sally and Molly for helping me to step back from my story and see it through the eyes of others.

Kip Mistral took me to task on every page. Her editorial guidance was a mighty fortress on which I could depend. Her passionate, earnest critique of the book greatly improved it. Kip, your unwavering objectivity was invaluable. All of my "voices" thank you.

Dr. Shannon Hayes threw out a lifeline just when I felt I was drowning in identity crisis. Her exhortations and input brought this book to life! Her perspectives were fresh, exhilarating, and exciting. Thank you, Shannon, for giving me the courage to be myself—all of it!

And many thanks to the WWOOFers—Jane Hamby, Jon Mikel Walton, and Sarah Fitzpatrick—who each shouldered enough of the load that I had the liberty of working on the manuscript every afternoon when I would otherwise have been "chopping wood and carrying water." And, of course, I am grateful to Jordan Hanson, who pours her very heart into my dreams and helps me make them come true!

I am also indebted to all of the people who came and went during those years on the farm. With every person came a teaching, a message, an insight. And, of course, there was the family with whom I shared the experience: Charlie, Jec, and Pher. Although we have all gone our separate ways over the years, our heart connection is indestructible. We shared something very special together.

I am also grateful to Vermont, all 9,250 square miles of it. Those rolling hills, bumpy gravel roads, and quaint general stores are forever imprinted in my soul. As the second least-populated state in the United States, it's the magnificently quirky place where I crossed the threshold into consciousness.

Notes

Chapter 1: Condemned to Be Free

1   Martin Heidegger (September 26, 1889–May 26, 1976) was a German philosopher whose *Sein und Zeit* (*Being and Time*) (1927) attempted to comprehend the meaning of "Being." His concept of *das Man* is often translated as "The They."

2   *Sinn des Seins* is the actual German phrase that Heidegger used for "sense of Being." It has been translated into English as *Being*.

3   Jean-Paul Sartre (June 1905–April 15, 1980) was a French existentialist whose *Being and Nothingness* represent his ideas about the concept of freedom.

4   *Bad faith* describes the phenomenon wherein one denies their total freedom by choosing to behave inauthentically.

5   See Denise Breton and Christopher Largent, *The Paradigm Conspiracy: How Our Systems of Government, Church, School, and Culture Violate Our Human Potential* (Center City, MN: Hazelden, 1996), 5.

Chapter 2: First Experiments in Freedom

1   See John de Graaf, David Wann, and Thomas H. Naylor, *Affluenza: The All-Consuming Epidemic* (San Francisco: Berrett-Koehler, 2005), 5.

Chapter 3: The End of Time

1   Maslow's hierarchy of needs is generally described as a pyramid on which the lowest level includes the most basic needs, while the more complex needs are located at the top. Needs at the bottom of the pyramid include the need for food, water, sleep, and warmth. The next level of needs are safety and security. Next comes love, friendship, and intimacy. And, finally, the need for personal esteem and feelings of accomplishment take priority.

2   See Richard Swenson, *Margin* (Colorado Springs: Navpress, 1992), 8.

3   Karen Horney, *Our Inner Conflicts: A Constructive Theory of Neurosis* (New York: W. W. Norton, 1992), 65.

4   See de Graff, Wann, and Naylor, *Affluenza*, 13.

5   Many Americans, including 37 percent of women earning less than $40,000 per year, get no paid vacation at all.

6   Edward Bernays, *Propaganda* (Brooklyn, New York: Ig Publishing, 2004), 71.

7   *The Century of the Self* is a BBC documentary film, produced by Adam Curtis, which chronicles the engineered rise of consumer culture. It was first screened in 2002 in four parts.

8   Benjamin Kline Hunnicut, *Kellogg's Six-Hour Day* (Philadelphia: Temple University Press, 1996), 4.

9   David Wann, *Simple Prosperity* (New York: St. Martin's, 2007), 46.

Chapter 4: Putting the Why and How Together

1   Viktor Frankl, *Man's Search for Meaning* (New York: Washington Square Press, 1984), 136.

2   Ibid., 165.

3   Gregg Easterbook, *The Progress Paradox* (New York: Random House, 2003), 317.

4   Madeline Levine, *The Price of Privilege* (New York: Harper Paperbacks, 2008), 8.

5   Abraham Maslow, "A Theory of Human Motivation," *Psychological Review* 50 (1943): 385.

Chapter 5: The New Stationary State

1   David Korten, *The Great Turning: From Empire to Earth Community* (San Francisco, CA: Berrett-Koehler Publishers, 2007).

2   Adam Smith (June 5, 1723–July 17, 1790) was a Scottish philosopher and a pioneer of political economics. Smith is the author of *The Wealth of Nations,* the first modern work of economics. Smith is widely cited as the father of modern economics.

3   John Stuart Mill (May 20, 1806–May 8, 1873) was a British philosopher who contributed significantly to social theory, political theory, and political economy. His conception of liberty justified the freedom of the individual in opposition to unlimited state control.

4   Joseph Hamburger, *John Stuart Mill On Liberty and Control* (Princeton, NJ: Princeton University Press, 1999), 31.

5   John Stuart Mill, *Principles of Political Economy* (London: 1889, 1923), 749–51.

6   Betsy Taylor founded the Center for a New American Dream, a nonprofit that helps Americans resist excessive commercialism and learn to consume responsibly to protect the environment, enhance quality of life, and promote social justice.

7   Eric Fromm, *The Art of Loving* (New York: Harper, 1956), 87.

8   United Nations Guidelines for Consumer Protection: Section G: *Promotion of Sustainable Consumption,* item #42.

9   Victor Turner, *From Ritual to Theatre: The Human Seriousness of Play* (New York: PAJ Publications, 1992), 33.

10   John Stuart Mill, *Principles of Political Economy.* (Amherst, NY: Prometheus Books, 2004), 514.

11   Ibid., 521.

12   We did not use the technique of *foal imprinting* on the farm. We preferred to allow the bond between mare and foal to be uninterrupted, and thus minimized human contact. We felt that this was a less invasive, more natural way to raise foals that honored the mare's role.

Chapter 6: The Spiritual Economy

1   Eric Butterworth, *Spiritual Economics* (Unity Village, MO: Unity Books, 2001), 102.

2   Ibid.

3   Joseph Schumpeter, *Business Cycles* (New York: McGraw-Hill, 1939), 39.

4   From the poem, "The Road Not Taken," by Robert Frost.

5   See John Stuart Mill, *Principles of Political Economy* (London, 1889), 751.

Chapter 7: Getting Out of the Fast Lane

1   Andrew Cohen, "If You're Conscious, How Can You Die?: An Interview with a Modern-Day Taoist Wizard Peter Ragnar," *What is Enlightenment?* 30 (September–November 2005): 18.

2   Ciji Ware, *Rightsizing Your Life* (New York: Springboard Press, 2007), 3.

Chapter 9: Halfway Up the Mountain

1   Herbert Marcuse (July 19, 1898–July 29, 1979) was a German philosopher, sociologist, and political theorist who, during the 1960s became celebrated as the "Father of the New Left."

2   In Jungian theory, the *Self* is the central guiding principle of the psyche, encompassing both the consciousness and unconscious of a person. The *ego,* on the other hand, is the waking center of self-reflective consciousness. The *persona* is the "mask" that a person presents to the world, while the *shadow* holds the parts of the self about which the person feels ashamed and guilty.

3   Herbert Marcuse, *One Dimensional Man* (Boston, MA: Beacon Press, 1964), 77.

4   Friedrich Wilhelm Nietzsche (October 15, 1844–August 25, 1900) was a nineteenth-century German philosopher.

5   The remaining 11 percent are what the survey calls need-directed, referring to Maslow's basic (physiological and safety) needs.

6   Michael Vannoy Adams, *The Mythological Unconscious* (New York: Spring Publications, 2009), 273.

7   The Übermensch is a concept in the philosophy of Friedrich Nietz-
     sche. Although there is no overall consensus regarding the precise
     meaning of the Übermensch, *Thus Spoke Zarathustra* presents the
     Übermensch as the creator of new values. In popular language,
     Nietzsche's Übermensch is called the Superman.

Chapter 10: The Wisdom of Insecurity

1   Jacques Rancière (1940–) is a French philosopher who was an early
     disciple of Marxist philosopher Louis Althusser.

2   Josef Pieper (May 4, 1904–November 6, 1997) was a German
     Catholic philosopher who wrote *Leisure: The Basis of Culture,*
     in which he attempted to recover a sense of leisure that was not
     a state of idleness but an occasion for activity beyond the field of
     servile work.

3   Josef Pieper, *Leisure: The Basis of Culture* (London: Faber and
     Faber, 1952), 17.

4   Victor Turner (May 28, 1920–December 18, 1983) was a British
     cultural anthropologist who wrote extensively on symbols, rituals,
     and rites of passage.

5   Victor Turner, *Blazing the Trail* (Tucson, AZ: University of Arizona
     Press, 1992), 54.

6   Consumer Price Index Report: October 30, 2009.

7   Alan Watts, *The Wisdom of Insecurity* (New York: Vintage Books,
     1951), 14.

Chapter 11: Behaving as if All Life Matters

1   Alexis-Charles-Henri Clérel de Tocqueville (July 29, 1805–April
     16, 1859) was a French political philosopher best known for his
     Democracy in America, in which he explored the effects of the ris-
     ing equality of social conditions on the individual and the state in
     western societies.

2   Bryan Walsh, "America's Food Crisis and How to Fix It," *Time
     Magazine,* August 31, 2009: 34.

3   Ibid., 35.

Chapter 13: Back to the Garden

1   Theodore Roszak (1933–) is professor emeritus of history at California State University at Hayward. A social critic, he was prominent in the development of the concept of ecopsychology.

2   Theodore Roszak, *The Making of a Counter Culture* (Berkeley: University of California Press, 1995), 38.

3   See Richard Tarnas, *The Passion of the Western Mind* (New York: Ballantine Books, 1991), 33.

4   Jean Gebser, *The Ever-Present Origin* (Athens, OH: Ohio University Press, 1986), 161.

Bibliography

Adams, Michael Vannoy. *The Mythological Unconscious*. New York: Spring Publications, 2009.

Bernays, Edward. *Propaganda*. Brooklyn, New York: Ig Publishing, 2004.

—————. 1947. "The Engineering of Consent." *The Annals of the American Academy of Political and Social Science* 250 (1947): 113–120.

Bowman, Carol. *Children's Past Lives: How Past Life Memories Affect Your Child*. New York: Bantam, 1998.

Breton, Denise, and Christopher Largent. *The Paradigm Conspiracy*. Center City, MN: Hazelden, 1996.

Buettner, Dan. *The Blue Zones: Lessons for Living Longer From the People Who've Lived the Longest*. Washington, DC: National Geographic, 2009.

Butterworth, Eric. *Spiritual Economics*. Unity Village, MO: Unity Books, 2001.

Capra, Fritjof. *The Turning Point: Science, Society and the Rising Culture*. New York: Bantam, 1984.

Cheeke, Peter R. *Contemporary Issues in Animal Agriculture*, third edition. New York: Vero Media, 2003.

Chopra, Deepak. *The Seven Spiritual Laws of Success*. Novato, CA: New World Library, 1994.

Cohen, Andrew. "If You're Conscious, How Can You Die?: An Interview with a Modern-Day Taoist Wizard Peter Ragnar." *What is Enlightenment?* 30 (September–November 2005): 18–26.

Dean, Brian. "The Puritan Work Ethic." *Business Magazine* (December 1996): 13–26.

de Graaf, John, David Wann, and Thomas H. Naylor. *Affluenza: The All-Consuming Epidemic.* San Francisco: Berrett-Koehler, 2005.

de Tocqueville, Alexis. *Democracy in America.* New York: Doubleday, 1969.

Dunn, Robert G. *Identifying Consumption: Subjects and Objects in Consumer Society.* Philadelphia, PA: Temple University Press, 2009.

Easterbook, Gregg. *The Progress Paradox: How Life Gets Better While People Feel Worse.* New York: Random House, 2003.

Frankl, Viktor. *Man's Search for Meaning.* New York: Washington Square Press, 1984.

Fromm, Eric. *The Art of Loving.* New York: Harper & Brothers Publishers, 1956.

Gebser, Jean. *The Ever-Present Origin.* Translated by Noel Barstad and Algis Mikunas. Athens, OH: Ohio University Press, 1986.

Gladstone, Malcolm. *The Tipping Point.* New York: Back Bay Books, 2002.

Hamburger, Joseph. *John Stuart Mill On Liberty and Control.* Princeton, NJ: Princeton University Press, 1999.

Heidegger, Martin. *Being and Time: A Translation of Sein and Zeit.* Albany, New York: SUNY Press, 1996.

Hicks, Ester and Jerry Hicks. *Ask and It Is Given.* Carlsbad, CA: Hay House, 2005.

Horney, Karen. *Our Inner Conflicts: A Constructive Theory of Neurosis.* New York: W. W. Norton, 1992.

Hunnicutt, Benjamin K. *Kellogg's Six-Hour Day.* Philadephia: Temple University Press, 1996.

Kealey, Daniel. *Revisioning Environmental Ethics.* Albany, New York: SUNY Press, 1987.

Korten, David. *Agenda for a New Economy.* San Francisco: Berrett-Koehler, 2009.

————. *The Great Turning: From Empire to Earth Community.* San Francisco, CA: Berrett-Koehler, 2007.

————. *The Post-Corporate World: Life After Capitalism.* San Francisco, CA: Berrett-Koehler, 2000.

————. *When Corporations Rule the World.* San Francisco, CA: Berrett-Koehler, 2001.

Levine, Madeline. *The Price of Privilege.* New York: Harper Paperbacks, 2008.

Lipset, S. M. "The Work Ethic—Then and Now." *Public Interest* 98 (Winter 1990): 43–47.

Macy, Joanna. *World as Lover, World as Self: Courage for Global Justice and Ecological Renewal.* Berkeley, CA: Parallax Press, 2007.

Marcuse, Herbert. *One Dimensional Man.* Boston, MA: Beacon Press, 1964.

Maslow, Abraham H. "A Theory of Human Motivation." *Psychological Review* 50 (1943): 384–389.

Mill, John Stuart. *Principles of Political Economy.* London, 1889, 1923.

————. *Principles of Political Economy.* Amherst, NY: Prometheus Books, 2004.

Narby, Jeremy. *Intelligence in Nature.* New York: Tarcher, 2006.

Packard, Vance. *The Hidden Persuaders.* New York: D. McKay, 1957.

————. *The Waste Makers.* New York: D. McKay Co., 1960.

Pieper, Josef. *Leisure: The Basis of Culture.* London: Faber and Faber, 1952.

Pink, Daniel. *A Whole New Mind: Why Right-Brainers Will Rule the Future.* New York: Riverhead Trade, 2006.

Ray, Paul H., and Sherry Ruth Anderson. *The Cultural Creatives: How 50 Million People Are Changing the World.* New York: Three Rivers Press, 2001.

Roberts, Paul. *The End of Food.* Boston, MA: Mariner Books, 2009.

Roszak, Theodore. *The Making of a Counter Culture.* Berkeley: University of California Press, 1995.

Saltmarsh, John A. *Scott Nearing: The Making of a Homesteader.* White River Junction, VT: Chelsea Green Publishing, 2008.

Schor, Juliet B. *The Overspent American: Why We Want What We Don't Need.* New York: HarperPerennial, 1999.

————. *The Overworked American: The Unexpected Decline of Leisure.* New York: Basic Books, 1993.

Schlosser, Eric. *Fast Food Nation*. New York: Harper Perennial, 2005.

Schumpeter, Joseph. *Business Cycles*. New York: McGraw-Hill, 1939.

Swenson, Richard. *Margin*. Colorado Springs: Navpress, 1992.

Tarnas, Richard. *The Passion of the Western Mind*. New York: Ballantine Books, 1991.

Tasch, Woody. *Inquiries into the Nature of Slow Money*. White River Junction, VT: Chelsea Green, 2008.

Turner, Victor. *Blazing the Trail*. Tucson, AZ: University of Arizona Press, 1992.

—————. *From Ritual to Theatre: The Human Seriousness of Play*. Second edition. New York: PAJ Publications, 1992.

Twenge, Jean M., and W. Keith Campbell. *The Narcissism Epidemic: Living in the Age of Entitlement*. New York: Free Press, 2009.

Walsh, Bryan. "America's Food Crisis and How to Fix It." *Time Magazine* (August 31, 2009): 11–27.

Wann, David. *Simple Prosperity: Finding Real Wealth in a Sustainable Lifestyle*. New York: St. Martin's Griffin, 2007.

Ware, Ciji. *Rightsizing Your Life*. New York: Springboard Press, 2007.

Watters, Ethan. *Urban Tribes: Are Friends the New Family?* New York: Bloomsbury USA, 2004.

Watts, Alan. *The Wisdom of Insecurity*. New York: Vintage Books, 1951.

Weber, Max. *The Protestant Ethic and the Spirit of Capitalism*. New York: Routledge, 2001.

Wilson, Eric G. *Against Happiness*. New York: Farrar, Straus and Giroux, 2009.

Index

About the Author

Sherry L. Ackerman, Ph.D., is a socially engaged philosopher who is passionate about sustainable, integrated lifestyles, voluntary simplicity, and animal spirituality. She credits Herbert Marcuse for having awakened her realization that she could be both an academic—a scholar—and a social catalyst—an activist. She lives the Good Life at Shastao Philosophical Hermitage at the foot of majestic Mount Shasta in Northern California.

For more information about her work, see: *www.sherryackerman.com* and *www.shastao.com.*

CPSIA information can be obtained at www.ICGtesting.com
Printed in the USA
LVOW06s0745281114

415882LV00007B/480/P